GRAVEN IMAGE

GRAVEN IMAGE

An Auto-biographical textbook

by

JOHN FARLEIGH

MACMILLAN & CO LTD

LONDON

1940

COPYRIGHT

CONTENTS

ACKNOWLEDGEMENTS

IT is a sad thing to read one's own letters of a few years back: they do not always do one credit. The mood of a letter is so transient that one hopes that one's own letters are burnt. I hesitated when asking for permission to print the letters that appear in this book, on this point of principle alone. The letters themselves, however, do so much credit to the writers that even they, I felt, would suffer no embarrassment at their reappearance. Besides, without them my book would be incomplete as a textbook.

And so I thank William Maxwell, Walter de la Mare, George Macy and Bernard Shaw for their permission to use their letters, and Bernard Shaw for his permission to reproduce his drawings, for which I have nothing but admiration.

Also must I thank Norman Weaver, who took the photographs with such care; and his models, the hands of those excellent engravers whose names appear in the section on wood engraving.

I do not know if it is etiquette to thank one's own publisher, but I will risk it. Whoever has this book must thank him for his generosity of production. Not one of the illustrations that I wished included has been cut down, and the list is formidable. Incidentally, his staff is excellent and has helped me in the task of making this book presentable. Their persistence, in view of the fact that war was declared half-way through, is an example of the great tradition of English publishing.   J. F.

CHAPTER I

ODD REFLECTIONS

WITH two hours to wait for a train, three tools and a spare block, I engraved my fourth block. It was accepted by the Wood Engraving Society, and from this I received my first commission to illustrate a book. And so I became engraver and illustrator.

By design or accident—who is to say? but the moral is obvious: always carry three tools and a spare block.

And so this record might end, and be used as an epitaph; but I have a desire to write a book about engraving and illustrating, though not another textbook. Engraving as an adventure! technique as a part of life! . . . it is not easy to say what sort of book I am hoping to write; but not another textbook. A record, perhaps, of engraving as I have discovered it, step by step; a record of labour that has been heartbreaking at times. A record of how a word or chance image has persisted in my mind, and emerged years later as a significant motif, just as a seed will appear months later and become the plant: emerge, perhaps, at some barren moment, renewing the whole quality of vision and revolutionizing technique.

I have no wish to make a survey of engraving, or to record its historical and technical development. I should be bored with the task of collecting data, referring to other textbooks, and repeating what others have said. I can write of the craft as I have found it and practised it, and no more. Because I write of engraving as a personal adventure, and because my discoveries are related to personal contacts and experiences, I must write this book as an autobiography.

Without going so far as Pangloss in thinking that all is for the best, I join him in tracing back events that appear to form a never-ending chain—so little in life seems to be unrelated.

If parts of this book seem irrelevant to engraving, I can only repeat that I am writing of technique as I understand it. The irrelevancies are myself, and it is through myself that I am writing of technique. My vision is coloured by certain experiences, and technique cannot be dissociated from them. A man's character is to be found in his handwriting. The artist's work is a portrait of his life, just as his life is a portrait of his work. Sad is the man who draws boots and shoes for a living. He must be for ever downcast.

The incident of to-day assumes the scale of a life-size canvas, and becomes a small vignette belonging to the past. The imagination, fed on these memories, discovers a sequence in them and evolves a theme which is released at a certain moment. The moment may be an odd one: the occasion of birth is not always preceded by trumpets—a king may pass through the guts of a beggar.

Did I always intend to be an illustrator and engrave wood? Of course not! How can the boy visualize the man when it is difficult for the man to visualize the boy? I find myself bewildered, and not a little alarmed, when I realize how little I have controlled my own actions. Perhaps, here and there, one has steered the course, but it is pathetic, and not a little humiliating, to realize the smallness of one's own contribution. Yet surely that small contribution is the miracle of man's progress. In the subtle web of life the smallest addition makes a complete rearrangement necessary. The unit returns to chaos for a while until time readjusts it. Thus is balance precariously preserved.

A chance remark can alter our conception of life. A chance discovery can upset the theories of the master mathematician. We grope for a while and then return to normal, perhaps more carefully or more appreciatively, but nevertheless normal to the new state of development.

The student is made to despair for days by a chance remark from his instructor. His recovery marks the return, not to the past, but to the normal. He has adapted himself to the new idea and for the moment is stabilized.

Reflections induce contemplation. Who looks at a house by the water without becoming hypnotised by its reflection? for this image, by being upside down, disconnects the mind from the insistent present to a world that does not obey the familiar rules. We are set free to wander through a series of apparently disconnected mental images. It is in such moments, when the normal control is relaxed, that the mind leaps forward to grasp the substance of an idea. The student of the house-upside-down-in-the-water comes back to reality a different man. Of such substance are dreams and fairy tales. Beware! lest, like Rip Van Winkle, you return to find you have lost your friends.

An old engraving or an old painting are reflections

of the past, the contemplation of which can send the artist into a number of different worlds according to his particular approach. This is the advantage and disadvantage of a Protean imagination. An artist is the inventor of new forms while appreciating the old forms. He can see technique and be blind to subject. He can be blind to technique and see only the beauty of forms. He may see nothing yet be sensitive to emotional content.

How many artists have wandered into the past and never returned! How many have seen the beauty of the early books and tried to return to them, only to find themselves in no-man's-land! A refuge is there, perhaps, but isolation is the condition of that refuge. Rip Van Winkle again.

The past is the past. Fatal to try to return. Fatal to contemplation to try to guide it. Fatal to imagination to give it grooves to work in. The reflection in the water is not for Narcissus. The lonely, awful spaces that are the world of creation are not for the weak.

There are no limitations to thought: only a craft has limitations and these must be constantly strained, for what we know of a craft is only what has already been said or done. Why should that knowledge be defined as limitations? Would Bewick or Blake have been great if they had accepted tradition only and gone no further?

But is there any limit to a craft? Dare I say, 'You must not do this—or that'? I can only say that perhaps it is straining the craft to make a graver imitate the texture of a chalk drawing or the quality of a pen line. This has been done in the past, but only by an effort of superhuman skill and patience, and because there was no other method of reproduction.

There are no limits to what can be done with the graver in the hands of the artist. Witness the history of the wood-block. Is there any period when development has stopped? Is there any country that has produced work exactly like another? As in painting; nationality, personality and period can be seen at a glance by the expert. The artist is limited by his personality, and nothing more.

The engravers of the last century, who so skilfully and laboriously imitated a pen drawing, were doing so because they were earning their living by reproducing another man's work. The wood-block was the popular method of reproduction, and so it developed into a highly skilled craft by force of circumstances. Towards the end of the 'nineties these engravers were fighting for their lives, making wood-engravings that were in close competition with the new rival—the halftone block. It was the swan song of reproductive engraving, and, if looked at with sensitive appreciation, a very beautiful one.

I cannot believe that these engravers were unaware of the beauty of their craft or its limitations. They knew their job so well and could ply it with such ease. Here and there, in the blocks that appear in such numbers in the periodicals of the nineteenth century, that seem dull and uninspired at first glance, one finds a square inch of creative engraving, where the engraver has admitted the impossible, and given up all efforts to imitate the drawing, that will be difficult to surpass.

And when all is said, and a block admitted to be dull and laboured, it possesses a beauty that puts a photographic reproduction to shame. Those engravers must have been a proud race of men, for they knew the beauty of highly skilled handwork. Look well at their engravings and you will find in them real men, living, suffering and dying. It is not possible to look at an original drawing of Leonardo's without getting the sense of contact that no mechanical reproduction will give, and these engravings, printed from the blocks as they were, are originals; they steam with the perspiration of their makers, and their work was well done. The sadness and beauty, and even the futility of their engravings, like the reflection in the water, possess us until we no longer see a trite illustration to an even more trite story. We pass into a world of shapes and tones, woven in the magic of white lines and delicate greys; through the whole fugue of accumulating tones and textures until we feel the very world must shake with the poignancy of this medium.

The men who made those engravings should be at rest, for there must be many who love them. There are a few of them alive to-day: gentle and noble men who deserve a better fate than that of struggling with starvation for lack of employment.

The calm surface of the water is disturbed. The reflections splinter and disappear. The normal world returns, but it is not quite the world we knew before. Now we see a receding wall of bricks as a lovely texture and a subtle gradation of tone. The magic lingers on into actuality, though we have said goodbye to the previous more placid existence that was less disturbed by beauty. There is a heavy price to be paid for everything, and when we have admitted this we are more able to stand the strain of knowledge: find exquisite beauty and it will discover the relentlessly ugly.

We are small vessels, when it comes to ecstasy, and can carry very little at a time. Witness the very sound suspicion of the arts shown by the average citizen. He knows, or at any rate suspects, the danger of flying too near the sun. Try to pull him part of the way with you and he will shuffle off uncomfortably. Wise citizen! For you is the labour of continuity. The steady sincerities of simple living cannot exist in the fungoid world of the imagination.

Repetition is the key to success.

A newspaper on the 'phone: 'Do you draw anything but black women?'

Myself: 'Oh yes—I've only drawn one black woman so far.'

Newspaper: 'We want you to illustrate a story with a brown girl in it.'

What a pity black girls do not appear in books as frequently as motor cars and erring husbands.

The reporters write: 'We are surprised to find Mr. Farleigh has not been to Africa.' The world is full of surprise for some people but not full of wonder.

I am asked: 'Did you know Bernard Shaw? Then how did you get his book to illustrate?' Oddly enough, I wonder that myself, though not for the same reason.

Labels—labels—labels, and a world that is canned. Be a man however virtuous and he makes one slip, he is drunkard, or licentious. Humpty Dumpty had a great fall, and all the king's horses and men couldn't put him together again. To draw a horse well the artist must wear riding breeches.

What! That scarecrow do good fashion drawings? Why not? Did Michelangelo paint the Sistine chapel in a top-hat? Did God make Sunday in His best suit?

Can men never achieve a status as the baboon has, and retain it? Is it the prerogative of man to be losing part of himself all the time, in the effort to find something better? Cannot he make an image that is satisfactory and see that it is good?

We lack adequate symbols nowadays. The artist once knew what a virgin looked like when he had to paint one, or at least he found a symbol that was recognized as such by his public. Now we only know stop—caution—go, stop—caution—go. We do not think all of the virgins on the walls of the National Gallery look like virgins. Does this mean that we are more discerning, or have we less faith?

I am asked why I became an engraver—no use my saying 'because I was trained as a painter'; and as I search back to find the reason, I find my attraction to wood-engraving was fostered by earlier experiences which began well before the incident at the opening of this chapter. That is why I have decided to make this book an autobiography in so far as I feel that certain experiences have affected my growth as an artist.

Other processes besides wood-engraving are described, for I have no desire to say that wood is the only medium fit to work in. I have described wax-engraving, for it is a beautiful process. When I was practising it between 1914 and 1918 it was already a dying craft and, for all I know, may have ceased to exist by now.

I write of things that interest me and that have affected my vision, and of the different crafts as they have helped me to express that vision. Whoever looks for technique in this book will find it only in patches. I leave it to the work of a future pedant to make a short technical treatise out of that which, with a little patience, will be found scattered throughout these pages.

1902

CHAPTER II

PRE-WAR

THE images become merged and simplified as they fade into perspective. A few accents stand out here and there, but these, too, are simplified to fit into the recession of the years.

Pre-war means childhood to those of my generation, and a complete unawareness of a disturbed political world. In the early years I remember making boundaries to my world of certain streets beyond which I dare not venture. Even to this day, when I am near those streets, I am aware of the same sense of discomfort that I felt as a child; the character I gave them remains.

The fields by Kensington Palace, in full view of St. Mary Abbott's spire, formed my playground, and any contact with beauty was made in the Palace, with its smell of the dust of the past and its gardens with their elegant ghosts.

I remember rolling down the slope, when the keepers were not about, that Queen Victoria must have rolled down as a child; and sliding on the Round Pond, that seemed to freeze more often in those days; and riding by the driver on a horse bus along Kensington High Street. I remember nothing of what I learnt at school, except that I enjoyed algebra, because it was pretty and because it was so convenient to know beforehand that x was the unknown quantity; and drawing, because I found it easy. At the age of twelve I informed my master that it was pointless for me to go on learning shorthand, having done sufficient to show that I could master it if I wanted

to. I said I was going to be a stained-glass artist, and that
I had no intention of going into an office, and so would
be better employed doing an extra drawing period. I
am still mystified that my explanation was accepted,
for I could have given no further details of my future,
as I do not remember having heard of stained glass.
Perhaps my attention had wandered in the choir, and the
windows suggested an interest apart from their intended
message. I became the envy of the class, not because I
was drawing, but because I was dodging shorthand.

About 1912 my background changed to the City, and
I was at once caught up by the magic of a place that
seemed teeming with purpose. At Kensington I had felt
the need of boundaries to protect me. The City, on the
other hand, seemed to invite exploration. The Inns of
Court established Dickens in my mind once and for all,
and I would search them for the characters he had
created, and loiter around the actual houses and offices
he had described so well.

Cruikshank had played no small part in my delight
and understanding of Dickens's world. I loved his vivid
characterization, though I was a little afraid of it too.

How many illustrators can transport a man or child
who knows nothing of the seduction of an etching or
engraving into a completely new world? In those days
Cruikshank made me see Dickens; and now I have the
added pleasure of appreciating the skill of his drawing
and etching.

What a test for an illustrator! Let him show his
illustrations to a man ignorant of craft, and then watch
for the reaction. No facility of handling will hide the
fact from the ruthless criticism of the innocent if the

VOTE
for
SPRUGGINS
Ten small
CHILDREN
and
A WIFE

BUNG
for
BEADLE
FIVE
SMALL
CHILDREN

VOTE
for
BUNG
INDEPEND

HASTE
to the
POLL

George Cruikshank

drawing has no content. He can thank God if the right idea gets across and ask for no more, for he may rest assured that if there is any alternative idea in his drawing that was not intended, that one will be discovered first.

The advertisers know to their cost the ability of the public to find an indecency in the simplest of statements of the most innocent of their goods; the illustrator must tell his own story if he does not want somebody else to tell it differently, or even embroider it.

I spent many Saturday mornings in a warehouse on the south side of the river where plate-glass was etched to embellish offices and pub windows. For a while I felt this was the stained glass I had thought about, and became thrilled by the skill of the men who painted the designs in Brunswick black, a preliminary to their being etched. They worked from tracings underneath the glass, but their speed and dexterity with the brush was a lesson in efficiency. I got as far as inquiring the wage of a beginner, and here a mist obscures my memory. For some reason I ceased to go there. The warehouse remains and the company's vans still go through the streets of London, though they are now motors and look much smarter. Every time I see one it stabs me with the thought that, but for some accident, I might be painting pub windows to-day.

On looking back, I realize how Fleet Street held me even then, with its almost theatrical air of excitement. The big newspaper offices, open night and day, and the continuous low thunder of the presses, seemed very friendly and proper.

By contrast, Ludgate Hill seemed artificial with its strangely assorted shops of expensive and dull presents.

Carpets, leather bags, wedding rings and an amusement fair all rolled into the smell of City lunches. It is probably the Oxford Street of the City and has changed very little to this day—indeed, what street does change its character unless it is completely rebuilt, which, fortunately, does not often happen?

I came into contact with what I realize now to be an advertising agency, and in early 1914 I became interested in the possibilities of drawing for advertising. Concern for my career led my parents to make inquiries, and I was told that I could get a job in one of the studios that served the agency. This studio was at Balham, and my heart sank. I did not know Balham, or it may have sunk still more, but I did realize my loss at not working in the exciting atmosphere of Fleet Street and the river.

Nevertheless, in June 1914, after certain interviews, I signed a contract, paid a premium and, at the age of fourteen, and with many headshakings of my head-master for dodging a scholarship, I became an articled apprentice for five years to the firm that is still known as the Artists Illustrators.

My first introduction to an oil palette was made here. Palettes were everywhere, though I am afraid they were only trade marks. There was one at the front gate in full war paint; this was a letterbox. Palettes seemed to be on every door, label, and letterheading. They created the atmosphere that I had missed in the Balham High Road, and I appreciated them as venerable symbols.

The studio itself was a strange building. It was two-storied with a flat roof and pseudo-Victorian battlements. On this roof was a glass studio for the photographic department, which made the second story. Below this, on the first floor, was the drawing office, which occupied the whole length and breadth of the building. The ground floor had two rooms. One seemed to have been used for a defunct craft, for it was derelict all the five years I was there. The other room, in which I had signed my indentures, was, I suppose, a sanctum for private business. It was seldom used, and always had the air of the best sitting room. It was a perfect imitation of what a photographer used to think an artist's studio ought to look like. A collotype of a semi-nude stood on a sadly over-ornamental easel. The few pieces of furniture were also pseudo and ornamental. A rather dim light came into this half-used, half-empty room owing to overhanging creeper. In the basement was a vast store of negatives in upright racks, and parcels of prints were packed in the rafters of the ceiling. At one end were long sinks for washing prints and preparing the plates for the wax-engravers, for wax-engraving was one of the many activities of the studio.

Some waste ground at the back formed a convenient playground for the lunch hour; while a long narrow lawn in front, just too small for tennis, set the house well back from the road. The lawn finished with a hedge and a tree at the front gate on which was fixed our biggest and brightest palette.

A strange retreat from the world, and so unlike the rest of Balham, and so far away from the laundry next door.

This laundry bought the studio after the War, when the firm could no longer afford it, as well as the printing press near by. Up to a year ago the shell remained visible from the train near Balham station. I looked for it a few weeks ago and found all traces removed;

a new brick building covered the site. The laundry is prospering.

Five years seemed a lifetime to me then, and the prospect of emerging, at the age of nineteen, a fully-trained commercial artist was remote and not to be brooded over. About this time I developed a strong desire to paint portraits—obviously the influence of so many palettes, and a photograph I remember seeing at the studio of a portrait by Alfred Stevens. I found the hours of eight till six none too long for the exciting things that had to be done. An hour's journey each way meant a twelve-hour working day, but it never occurred to me that I might do better with my time. I started each day with dusting the studio, and raised no objection to this at first as it gave me ample opportunity of looking round at the various jobs in hand. At nine o'clock on the first day I was given a desk and a page of type to copy. Cheltenham Bold has a nostalgic quality to me even now. Until midday I measured with dividers and ruler and drew the forms of the letters with a careful eye to character. I was placed under the care of an old man, who is now dead and, I hope, in the heaven he used to talk to me about. I was to get to know him very well in the near future, when the War emptied the studio of all but the two of us. He had a passion for music and spent some time in curing me of whistling: a habit I found difficult to abandon, for I was very happy.

After the first few haphazard days I was given a time sheet that mapped out my programme for the day. Each hour was devoted to one of the many different crafts that the studio practised; thus a general education was ensured before I began to specialize.

C

My day's work included lettering, wax-engraving, typing (pressing type into the hot wax of an engraved plate), building the mould on the wax plate, map construction (most of the wax-engravings were of maps, which had to be constructed before engraving), and black-and-white drawing for press advertisements. Odd periods were filled in with clearing drawers of large maps into some sort of order, cleaning up and preparing plates for wax-engraving and looking up originals of old press drawings that had been stored and docketed. Parts of these would be used again on the new advertisement, and I have often seen a drawing go up to be photographed in such a flimsy condition, owing to patching up, that it had to be put between glass to hold it together. Whether this saved time in the end I never found out, but it seemed to be the tradition then. I doubt if such a procedure would be possible now, as fashion changes quicker than it did in 1914.

With my time so broken the first few weeks went by very quickly.

I learned to overcome my horror of using the telephone, and to pack a good parcel with a slip-knot. I learned to save all paper and string from incoming parcels, and to keep a faithful record of my activities on a time sheet. These habits I have preserved to the present day; I judge the quality of the parcels I receive by my ability to use the paper and string again. Method and economy in all things are habits, and habits are a part of every craft. Through them we learn to love materials: the smell of printing ink and oil; the noise and chatter of printing presses; the aloofness of a tool when it is lying idle and its adaptability when it is in the

hand, waiting on you and whispering to you. The tool
has a subtle voice. It will only confide in the understanding craftsman. It needs as much grooming as any
great beauty. It can become the only living thing about
you. All feeling and life; all action and intensity can
pass into the tool until the body clouds up and only the
point of the tool is in focus. It is then that the tool will
talk and all is well.

So much for early training and habits acquired.

In perspective, I can thank the man who taught me
how to pack a parcel when my ideas were of stained
glass and portrait painting. At the time I resented giving
so much time to jobs that seemed so unrelated to drawing. I was proud of my indentures and scorned the work
of odd job boy. I was to get a still wider training and
resent it even more, for six weeks after I had started
most of the men in the studio went off to Territorial
Camp for their annual training; they never returned,
for War was declared during that fortnight and they
quietly disappeared before I had got to know them well.
Only one of those men came back after the War. I
hardly recognized him and was afraid to approach him,
for what he had been through had turned him to a mask
that seemed to forbid any approach. It is possible we
were both afraid of one another.

July 1914

CHAPTER III

AUGUST 1914–JUNE 1918

THE enormous crowd gathered round the Houses of Parliament seemed to me to be without purpose; waiting for something that it did not quite understand—a sort of puzzled-dog feeling, combined with a queer prescience of the next few years.

War was declared and the tension relaxed.

It meant very little to me, and everybody was confident it would be over in three months. One felt the Army and the Navy were somewhere, waiting to take on jobs of this sort. Apparently the Belgians were affected, for in the early days one saw men raising their hats to refugees.

The immediate effect, as far as I was concerned, was apparent in the studio. Work was still flowing in but half the staff had gone. As an apprentice I should have being doing practice work for at least a year. Owing to our shortage of staff I was given professional work to do in the first few months. From then on I practised on actual jobs. If the work was not as good as it should have been, what could be expected?—there was a war on and nothing else was very important. The studios were lucky who had kept on old men or had acquired young apprentices ready to take over.

For a while, a few men, eligible for the Army, carried on at the studio; conscription was some way off and recruiting had not yet become an embarrassing part of daily life. Whenever possible I referred to the schedule that had been made out for me in my first week and continued practice work, but as more men became affected and left, I slowly abandoned all idea of keeping to my programme: I did whatever job was on hand at the moment.

And so I came into close contact with Donald Macbeth, the presiding genius of the firm. I must have been a trial to him with my many protests, for I learned the lesson of adapting myself to war conditions very slowly. Many a time when I complained of the odd jobs I had to do, which to me seemed beneath my dignity as a draughtsman, he would talk patiently of the difficult state the firm was in. On one occasion, when I point blank refused to clean out the lavatory, he did it himself with complete lack of ostentation.

It took me a long time to understand him, for he was an eccentric man. He had great personal charm, however, that always sent me back to my job in a better frame of mind.

It was he who sent me to an evening class at Bolt Court to learn to draw. It was he who talked of drawing as a means of expression. He breathed enthusiasm and culture into what might have become an ordinary workshop, and he had a sadness for beauty that I did not fully understand at the time. It was he who taught me how to wrap a parcel and how to talk to people. Because he knew a good painting he could enthuse about the collotype he had made of it; and there were few to touch his collotype work in those days.

I meet him occasionally in London, and he still runs the business. He is, as usual, walking in the rain and cold with no hat or overcoat. He told me, on one occasion when we met, that he had never worn an overcoat as it made his head ache, and he always lost his hat if he used one. I could never understand this eccentricity when I was young, which shows how easily we can misunderstand for want of a simple explanation. I used to think he scorned to wear such things, and accordingly felt inferior for having to do so myself.

He is a wise, cultured man, and his sadness for beauty, which I understand now, is more pronounced.

I am sure he sent me to an art school to learn to draw because he loved drawing; and that he knew it would be my gain as well as his. Thus he started a habit for me, of going to evening classes, that lasted for the next ten years: five while I was an apprentice; three while I was a day student, and the two years while I was teaching at Rugby. The habit of working in the evening is difficult to break to this day.

On my first evening at Bolt Court in 1914 I sat astride a 'donkey' for the first time with the conviction that nobody was happier than myself. The next two and a half hours were my own; I had a good light and a cast of two pears and some leaves. I remember the drawing did justice to my feelings. It was stippled with loving care and provoked the interest of the excellent lady who was teaching there. She asked me if I was a lithographer, and so I heard of lithography for the first time, and for ever after connected it with a carefully shaded drawing of pears. After that first reference I was to remain unenlightened on the crafts for many years, apart from those I learnt at the studio, but I was not anxious to do anything else but draw at the art school. It always seemed, from the very beginning, that drawing was more important than craft.

I am certain now that a craft can be learnt in a single night compared with the job of drawing. Craft is the tail of drawing and should wag in its proper place—about eighteen inches behind. Sad is the dog with a tail that wags in front of his nose, for he must be so conscious of it.

The English are craftsmen at heart and tend to become too skilful. The arts get choked with craft. The academician is so dull but so damnably skilful; he knows his job so well. If only we had one word for craft and drawing as the French have for drawing and design. There is no essential difference between the act of a tool and the act of a pencil.

Planks of wood, planes in sculpture, illusion of planes in drawing, contours, tones, colour, emotional stress in design, all are achieved by using a tool.

A good artist is sensitive to the dictates of his tools, and uses them with restraint. He does not shout, nor does he wear his heart on his sleeve. There is no need, for in the quiet subservience of his craft to his art is a song that makes ostentation unnecessary.

I was to discover quietness in many things as the War progressed. The few men we had left at the studio disappeared quietly, and their subsequent death was discussed quietly and in few words. I found myself working through the long hours with the one man left, who was too old to contemplate any kind of war service, and the days went by quietly.

I did a fair amount of wax-engraving, for the drawing department was very slack. Publicity had gone into other fields. People were no longer asked to buy so much as to give.

'Your king and country need *you*', the posters would say, and point a terrible finger.

I was now carrying a job through until it was finished. The discipline of working on one job for days on end, and sometimes weeks, was, no doubt, good for me in the long run, but at the time it was a severe strain. There were days when I would have rushed out of the room with hate for the job I was doing that tied me to a desk, while the trains, that I could see from the window, were rushing to and fro.

I formed a resolution very early in my apprenticeship that I would become a free-lance artist. And now that I am one, I find the discipline a valuable asset for those jobs that take months and sometimes years to complete. The endurance necessary to hold on to a job for any length of time is entirely a matter of training.

Free lance is an ironic term. It means that one works all hours of the day and night, and is paid only at intervals instead of weekly.

In 1916 my ambition to paint portraits in oils was abandoned for a desire to paint water-colours. Fired by some Girtins that had been sent to us to photograph, I longed to paint old gateways, bricks, and ruins with creeper.

The old man working with me was an enthusiastic water-colourist. He gave me lessons in the lunch hour that stopped most punctually at one minute to two o'clock, and I succeeded in producing a fair copy of an old bridge and its reflection in the water—I regret to say that this water-colour was most carefully framed and hangs upon a certain wall to this day.

I had ample time for reflections. While I was developing my skill at wax-engraving more or less mechanically, I was solving the problems of my world. Since most of these problems were unrelated to work they need not be discussed at any great length here, but running strongly through my mind was the idea of doing something other than sitting at a desk from eight till six, working on jobs that, though interesting, gave no room for self-expression. I was not fully conscious of this at the time, since I do not remember having anything particular to express, unless a desire to see real things and say something about them—though what to say I had no idea—can be said to be an incipient stage of the creative disease. Of one thing I am certain: I showed no imagination in my work. Everything I did was well within the limits of what was required. I accepted the popular conceptions of everything, and therefore ran no risk of making a drawing that would offend a client or even make him uneasy. A blissful state! The magic of Holman Hunt's *Flight into Egypt;* the beauty of the lady so chastely shaven and semi-garbed in veils by the marble pool; the sickly pall of the sea giving up its dead, and the fair Ophelia who was most obviously under water, if not quite dead. [Didn't the model catch a bad cold because the water was not heated one day during a sitting? (floating?)]

Was I adolescent or were those artists adolescent? I confess that I am still rather intrigued with the *Death of Chatterton* when I pass it in the Tate. And so my introduction to painting consisted of a few visits to certain sections of the Tate Gallery and brooding over various illustrated

Academy catalogues some considerable number of years
out of date.

Perhaps these pictures were stirring my imagination
in some way, for in 1919, when I was first moved to
paint in oils, I painted (in my mind) a large canvas
showing the death of Shelley. I saw how the water
could be shown dripping off his clothes as the kindly
spirits lifted him gently from the water, while the pre-
mature glow of a funeral pyre on the distant shore gave
the right pallid-spiritual role to the figure relaxing across
the canvas. While this painting filled my mind I was
dragging new clean hoghair brushes across new clean
canvas and looking at the new tubes of paint, appreciating the shape of the filled tubes and the oily smell
of the paint inside. Such lovely tools had to be played
with before spoiling. I played with them long enough
to outlive the desire to paint the death of Shelley, and,
as far as I remember, copied a vigorous painting of the
Italians attacking somebody in the Great War.

But I am anticipating, and must revert to 1916 and
wax-engraving, for it deserves mention. As far as I
know, there is no exact description of this craft on
record, and as I feel it could be revived and modernized
I propose to discuss it in detail. And so I warn the reader
that if he likes he may skip the next section.

Wax-engraving is a method of obtaining a perfect
line block without the use of a camera or chemicals to
take the virtue out of the lines. The clarity of the print
can only be rivalled by that of the wood-block. We
used it almost entirely for maps, plans, and drawings of
machinery, but I have it in my mind to revive it some
day and use it freely and for other purposes. I remember

seeing some large American plates, engraved but not yet made up into moulds, that were exquisite examples of cartography. There were very few firms still engraving in England, and it was generally recognized that the Americans were far ahead of us in the beauty of their technique.

The first stage is a long, laborious, and rather dreary one of cleaning the brass plate with pumice stone to remove all scratches—it pays to be careful with the plates beforehand and not dig holes in them—and then give a final polish with a smooth stone; it gives the mind plenty of opportunity to wander, and there is a lot to be said in favour of this. The polished plate is then stained a dusky black with a solution of nitrate of silver. When dry there should be no free sediment on the plate—a touch with the finger will show whether the black will come off.

The wax ground to be applied to the plate should be prepared beforehand, as a fairly large quantity should be made and the making needs careful supervision; the ultimate perfection of the engraving depends upon the right consistency of the wax.

I always enjoyed preparing the wax for the ground, partly because it has the satisfactory sensation of cooking and partly for the journeys to Price's Candle factory at Battersea, where the wax, both for the ground, which was hard, and for building the mould, which was soft, was obtained. I enjoyed nosing round a different kind of workshop, and the queer processes going on made the strange smells bearable. (The Exhibition at Wembley justified itself when it revealed the secret of how the letters got into peppermint rock.)

The harder wax, that formed the basis of the ground, is melted down, and zinc white, in powder form, is added. When the mixture has been well stirred it is poured into a mould consisting of a printing chase in reverse position on a slab of metal. When almost cool, cut into strips with a knife and lift off the chase. The wax can then easily be removed in sticks about 6 in. long, 1 in. wide and ½ in. thick.

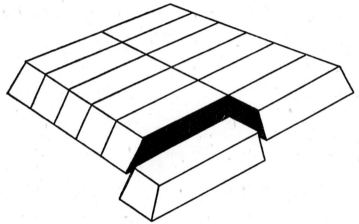

After chase has been removed and wax cut.

The final appearance of the stick of wax is a very smooth, almost opaque white, sufficiently hard to offer considerable resistance when scratched with the finger-nail. The zinc white powder cannot be too finely ground. If the wax is at all granular owing to coarse powder it will break away during engraving.

The ground is applied by heating the plate on a tank (similar to that used in etching), and passing a stick of the wax over the plate in horizontal and vertical lines.

The wax is distributed evenly by means of a comb that works in spirals across the plate, this action being repeated in different directions.

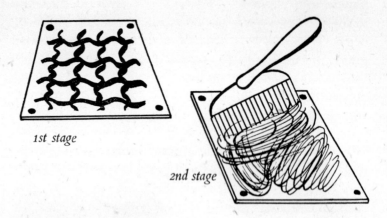

1st stage

2nd stage

While still hot the plate is held by two hooks from the holes in opposite corners of the plate and shaken in a half-circle backwards and forwards while keeping the plate horizontal.

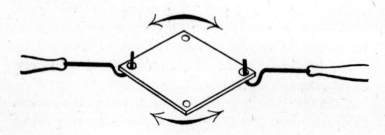

This smooths out the ground by centrifugal force and thins it at the same time—the surplus wax heaping up on the edge and flying off if too much has been put on. The plate is now ready for use. The ground should appear almost opaque—the blackened plate just showing through the white—and thin enough for the tool to be hardly conscious of the wax as its cuts through to the metal surface below.

We always kept a store of these prepared plates in negative racks by the side of each bench, and the engraver selected a plate suitable for the job in hand—the thicker grounds being kept for the simpler drawings. A brown print was made of the drawing to be engraved, and this was black-leaded on the back for tracing purposes. Any drawing on thin paper would do as well. We used photographs, as many of the drawings of machinery came in ready for engraving and the originals had to be preserved. It took me a long time to get a clean tracing, for I did not always prepare the back with sufficient care. The surplus lead should be rubbed off with cotton wool and rubbed down until no lead comes off on the wool. The print is made fast on the plate by touching various points on the edge with a hot tool. The wax melts locally and holds the paper firm and the design is traced down with a metal tracing point or hard pencil.

A bunsen burner is a very necessary part of a wax-engraver's equipment. A false line can be removed by redistributing the wax with a hot tool, the earlier process of grounding the plate being repeated locally.

If the plate is a large one a hole is cut in the attached print and engraving commenced where the wax is laid bare. Thus the major part of the plate is protected by the print, which shows at the same time the drawing—unlike the old method of making a highly finished life drawing and working through a similar hole cut out of blank white paper mask.

This tool is used in different widths for all straight
lines, tints, curves and circles. For straight lines a metal
T-square is necessary, curves being made with a French

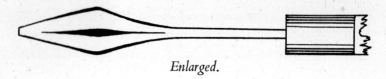

Enlarged.

curve, and for circles the tool is put in a compass. The
tool is dragged from left to right and the cutting face is
kept flat to cut its full width clean through the wax to
the metal plate. A wide line is not easy to cut clean. The
angle of the tool must be ninety degrees from north
and south, and about sixty degrees east.

Top view of tool showing angle.

If the tool does not remove all wax from the line the
result will be a faulty electro.

If the tool scratches into the metal the electro will be
faulty and the plate difficult to polish again.

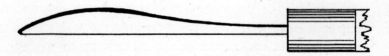

This tool is used for freehand lines. Held like a pen,
it is sharpened to give an even thickness of line in whatever direction it moves. It can be sharpened to give any

thickness of line and must make a perfect contact with the metal plate. This applies to every tool, and practice and experience at holding each tool at the right angle is necessary before it is achieved.

Rivers on maps, shown by a line that thickens gradually towards the sea, are drawn with a hard pencil held vertically. To thicken the line the point is rubbed down a little; the final thickness at the end is arrived at through many stages of thickening the point.

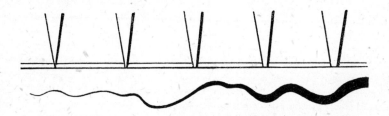

Flat line tints for shaded areas are put in with a ruling machine that controls the spacing of the lines but not their length, the tool being put down at the beginning of the line and lifted off at the end by hand. This means that an irregular shape can be tinted with perfect precision.

The diagram is not a complete drawing of the machine, but is given to clarify the description of its function.

The two long runners permitted the whole of the superstructure to slide backwards and forwards (I use the past tense as this particular machine may be obsolete now). The tool seen resting on a plate was fixed in a screw-holder that was hinged to the centre block, thus permitting the tool to be lifted up and down when

D

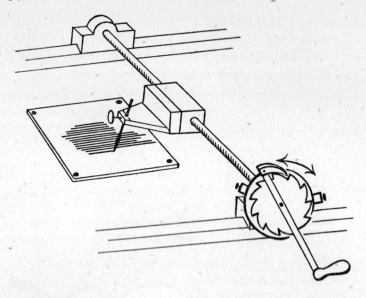

necessary. The centre block was built on the thread of the crossbar, and the revolution of this crossbar moved the block along in position for the next line. The width between the lines was controlled by a ratchet-wheel on the near side that could be set to the required width. The direction of the tint was controlled by altering the angle of the plate under the tool. This machine was sensitive and had to be nursed with great care if a perfect tint was to be achieved. Relax for one moment and a line went wrong.

Unfortunately, the more perfect your tint the more noticeable is the slightest error; what a shocking moral could be drawn from this. Besides, regularity and perfection belong to the dull things on the whole, and should be aimed at but never achieved.

But in some things regularity and perfection are

necessary. The machine supplies these things so we cannot break them up or discard them. They have beauty too, for men have become attached to them; and, moreover, they can be made to make beautiful things. In particular, this ruling machine did make beautiful tints, even if it were a little fallible—an irritating rather than an endearing quality in a machine. A regular engraved tint is a lovely thing. A tone produced by a series of lines has a life and quality that no wash or halftone has; and the direction of the line can contribute not a little to the significance of the drawing; a glance at Bewick's *Fables* will convince anybody on that point. If overdone, flat tints can become dull, but when used sparingly and in the right place they can add dignity as well as correctness to a design.

A man in mourning would not wear even a scarlet pimpernel in his coat, but under happier circumstances such decoration would be considered most restrained. Accent in all things must be related to the circumstances.

The tints on my maps, however, were only decorative by accident: their object first and foremost was function. Distinctive tints had to be evolved to make certain areas quite separate from others. I have no doubt that the outlook that this kind of work developed has been useful to me in using tints and textures in wood-engraving in a functional sense rather than in a sprawling decorative manner. The attractive, decorative quality of the textures possible in wood-engraving is a trap to many artists, and drawing can be lost only too easily by over-indulgence in this direction.

Cross-hatching on the wax plate was successful when the ground was good—if it broke away then woe betide the apprentice who had laid the ground, he would be wise to slip out on an errand.

To cross-hatch, a tint is first laid in one direction and the plate turned round in the ruling machine for the second tint to be cut across. It is possible to get any number of colours by overprinting these tints, and often the colours were very beautiful indeed, especially when combined with black.

I was surprised to find how much practice was necessary to make a good tint, and ultimately how sweetly the work would flow when I had mastered the technique.

Imperfect technique is so often pardoned on æsthetic grounds. If we face the truth, it is generally clumsiness or incoherence, sometimes lack of experience. This latter has a certain charm; we find it in all young and inexperienced things—children, puppies, or colts. The poetry of child language comes from a limited vocabulary. Their drawings are almost always successful because they have so little to say and their craft is negligible and does not concern them. Often this lack of craft is mistaken for freshness of vision—it is fresh, of course, to the jaded adult mind that is either over-trained or over-sophisticated. The artist must beware lest his artistic voice lose touch with his craft—it is the loss of his tail. So much emotional daubing that is done might be called Manx art; as bad to have no tail, as all tail.

There was no lenient standard of æsthetic appreciation when my tints on the maps went wrong; the plate was either balled up or could be corrected by hours of patient labour, and these hours had to be accounted for on the time sheet that lay for ever at one's elbow.

When all line work, freehand and ruled, was completed, the names of towns, etc., were put in with type. This was a skilled job and full of danger.

The plate was put on a tank heated by gas jets inside.

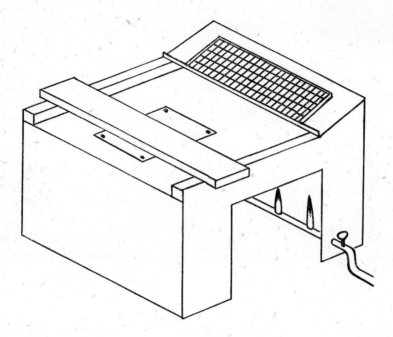

It was my job to light these in the morning, and when I first started I was shown how to do it with awful warnings, which were justified by the experience of one of the men who lost his eyebrows and half his hair by carelessly turning on the gas too soon before lighting. This was not the only danger. If the tank became too hot the engraving would melt under your eyes—I have seen a week's work disappear in a moment.

The name of a town was set up in a small holder, the base of the type being cushioned on the rubber band to give resiliency. The type was held in position by the

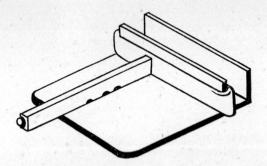

fingers and the holder placed vertically against the rest. It was then lowered to touch the wax plate and rocked gently from side to side until the type insinuated itself through the hot wax to the plate beneath.

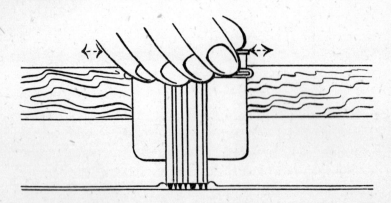

Again a clean impression is essential and can only be achieved with practice.

If a name had to be curved or shaped, it was put in
letter by letter—this being the only occasion I know of
when such a thing can be done with type; it meant that
one could give type the consideration in spacing that is
usually associated with the drawn letter. Each letter
throws up a slight ridge of displaced wax around it, and
the slight break around all type that crosses a line or tint
is one of the distinctive marks in identifying a wax-
engraving.

Dotted tints were put in with fullpoints or colons
and could be graded by using different types.

Battered type was discarded as it was discovered, as
it was often the cause of a slip, and a slip across the plate
meant hours of patching and subsequent inventiveness
on the time sheet. A slip can occur from the plate being
too cool—the extra pressure needed to get the type
through the cool wax making the chances of a slip far
more likely.

A faulty impression was removed by local regrounding
with a hot engraving tool—if the word was over a tint
it was not so good, as the tint had to be re-entered, and
the machine was not happy on this job: it was not easy
to replace the plate in the exact position on the bed.

The final stage is now reached and the wax mould is built up on to the engraved plate.

The wax used for this is soft and prepared in a similar fashion to the ground apart from the zinc white, which is unnecessary.

The pen used to control the flow of wax is a copper coil on a handle with a piece of bent wire running through the centre core. The coil controls the flow of the wax and the wire acts as a nib does to ink.

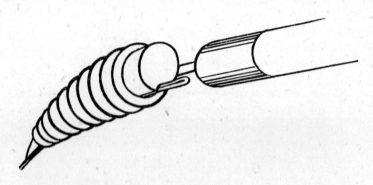

The pen is heated in a bunsen burner and the degree of heat is regulated according to the rapidity of the flow of wax required. The wax is pressed against the top of the coil and emerges along the wire nib as a thin stream. This stream is guided round the edges of each line or letter where there is a space large enough to need building up.

It is a reverse process to wood-engraving, where the white spaces have to be sunk.

When all lines are thus protected, the pen is heated to obtain a fuller flow of wax. This makes a high mound of wax that joins up to the shallow banks that have already been made. As the spaces become bigger the mounds of wax must become higher.

If the pen gets too hot or the flow too great the work is flooded and has to be re-entered!

In appearance the finished job shows the engraved lines sunk in a bed of wax—a sort of quilted effect.

An electro is then grown on to the mould and the line block emerges.

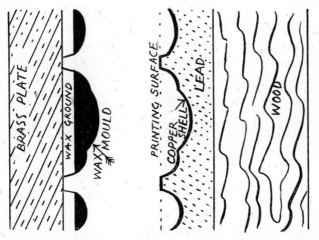

Section through mould of wax engraved plate and electro.

The mould is then returned from the block-makers in a disgusting condition. It is heated and scraped clean of wax, and the process of pumice-stoning starts all over again to prepare the brass for another engraving. The life of a brass plate is indefinite.

It is a craft that might well be revived. If any block-maker can remove the necessity for building the wax mould—the only laborious and uneconomic part—it could be used for almost any kind of drawing and would make better line blocks than can be made via the camera.

The pen-and-ink draughtsmen of the last century would have given anything for such a process, for the quality of their drawings would have been preserved, instead of being submerged into wood-engraving: while the modern artist, still groaning under the tyranny of the present line block process, would welcome such a direct process.

With practice an artist should be able to draw as freely on the wax plate as an etcher does, and if the block could be made direct at this stage with no wax mould to be built the result would be a facsimile of his drawing on economic lines.

Running a curious parallel to wax-engraving was the swelled gelatine process that we used for making line blocks from highly modelled pencil drawings—mostly studies of fish, birds and such like for scientific books.

The original drawing was made on a specially grained paper—probably as fine, or finer, than the finest half-tone screen. The effect was that of an exquisitely stippled drawing, the tones ranging from imperceptible greys to rich blacks.

This drawing was transferred in some way (I could never extract the secret from our photographer) on to gelatine, and on this gelatine the image could be seen swelled up in relief. Black wax was poured on to this gelatine image by placing a chase in reverse over the gelatine and filling it with the wax. When the chase was removed and the wax mould lifted, the gelatine was peeled off, leaving the image now sunk into the surface of the wax block.

From then onwards the process of building up a wax mould, from which the electro was made, was similar to that in wax-engraving; the only difference being that it is a much more difficult business to build up a wax mould on another wax mould than on a cold metal plate. I was often called in to build them when our photographer (who usually built these moulds and, for some reason, was an expert) was too busy; and a nightmarish job I found it. The cold plate of the wax-engraving made the control of the flow of hot wax fairly easy; on the black wax moulds it was only possible to keep control by lowering the temperature of the building pen and keeping the wax flow well in hand. I have often, in a moment of absent-mindedness, heated the pen too much, and seen the hot wax flood over the image, and that spells disaster, for there is no way of recovering the drawing as in wax-engraving.

I remember dashing a tool over a mould in sheer exasperation on one such occasion, when I had nearly finished a rather intricate piece of building.

It is, like wax-engraving, another way of producing a perfect relief block; by having no intervening chemical process the original virtue of the drawing is preserved; but also, like the wax-engraving, the process of building up the mould needs replacing before it can be successfully revived to suit modern conditions.

I acquired the necessary skill for these processes very slowly, and only in the course of the next few years. This was partly due to the variety of work that we handled; every kind of job that came in had to be done by myself or the one other man.

In spite of this variety of work I remember an acute sense of monotony, caused, no doubt, by the long regular hours and lack of companionship—when the old man was away ill or on holiday I was entirely alone in the drawing office. This monotony was only interrupted by the growing apprehension that the war was going on in just the same way that I was getting older, and that I should ultimately get drawn in and disappear in my turn, just as everybody else had disappeared.

At one period, when the drawing office was slack and photography booming, I spent a few months upstairs in the photographic studio making silver prints (one never seems to see these lovely prints now), developing rotographs, making wet plates, and even getting as far as dry plates, and I can still see the long map of the Rhine that we pasted together showing good bombing points coloured in red.

I spent a few weeks 'laying-on' for a collotype machine round at the printing works; trying to find out the process from the ever-secretive craftsman.

At the studio we continued to handle every kind of job that came along: pen drawings of famous men; rolls of honour—including the Japanese and Italian flags; designing bookplates; touching-up photographs and turning out occasional advertisements for silk under-wear—although these became rare as the war went on.

One day the silence of the studio was shattered by my companion asking me if I read books. I confessed, and he forthwith made a list of books that I should read, and so I started my acquaintance with the English writers, and incidentally the painters, of the eighteenth century. Thackeray's *English Humorists* and *The Four Georges* headed the list, and I plunged into a new world and found Hogarth, whom I have since recognized as the father of Cruikshank—the one illustrator I knew well at that time.

And so with discussions on music my education was nursed, with a grave warning not to paint on Sundays or draw from the nude—with the instance of the very great artist who promised his mother he would never practise either, and especially the latter.

I am afraid I ignored the warnings: Sunday was the only day left for painting, and I automatically accepted the nude as part of the business of drawing. I fear the old gentleman was much more interested in my first drawing from the nude, when I showed it to him, than I was.

I discovered more about London than I should have done in the ordinary way, owing to the fact that the war had killed off even our odd job boy, who, at eighteen, had joined up, to be killed in a few weeks. The delivery of drawings to block-makers, and parcels to various warehouses, gave me an extensive insight into the curious workshops of London; they always seem to be made up of wooden partitions and dark staircases and doors through which came the hum of machines and the smell of industry.

These glimpses of strange trades were as exciting to me as the peeps behind scenes that I got by hanging round the backs of theatres for hours during my weekends.

I booked a seat at the Lyceum to see the Carl Rosa
Company do *Tales of Hoffman*, and revelled in an
atmosphere that I did not understand. I understood
nothing of the opera or the music, and when, in an
interval, a young enthusiast beside me said 'Don't you
adore "The Night of Stars"?' I replied that I hadn't seen
it, which I suppose was correct, for I had heard it
during the previous scene but had not known it.

Certain periods of that four years seem to have slipped
by with nothing happening. I would spend my lunch
hours in the tree overlooking the road, and in a cloud
of leaves watch unsuspecting passers-by with a mind as
blank as is humanly possible.

And then the awful day when the observation balloons
that hung suspended in front of my window, day by
day, until they seemed fixtures, broke loose, and the
balloons floated helplessly above with black specks
clinging to the wires. The men fell off a few minutes
later, we were told, but I can only hope that it was yet
one more legend of the war that came into being so
easily in those days.

Apprehension of the Army was quickened by air
raids; living in the City gave one ample experience.
The first raid over London by Zeppelins resulted in a
row of warehouses near St. Paul's being burned down.
I saw St. Paul's lit up a brilliant red and produced one
of my first posters, intended for a fire insurance company.
It was returned with the comment that publicity was
too expensive an indulgence at that moment. Not to be
daunted, I returned a letter to the effect that it may
become more expensive if the war went on, perhaps it
would be better to 'do it now'—a phrase that was in the

air. The grim reply came back: 'If the war goes on much longer we shall not need publicity of any kind.'

'Keep the home fires burning!'

The air raids increased, and destroyed sleep; it was often difficult to keep awake in the long quiet days at the studio. When aeroplanes replaced the Zeppelin the disturbances occurred earlier; often as early as six-thirty in the evening. On these occasions I preferred to be caught at the art school than spend the time in the cellar at home. Such family gatherings may be good for the consanguineous affections, but my fear was dispelled more by the crowd of students than by the tense waiting in the cellar. If the alarm was given while I was on my way to Southampton Row I would run for it rather than return home.

One evening, walking up Kingsway (which was hardly built in those days), the sky became brilliant with a whitish red glare and a shattering explosion followed. I found myself crouching with another man in opposite corners of a doorway, waiting for more to follow. I heard later that it was the awful Silvertown explosion, where an ammunition factory had blown up; then nightmare stories of Blackwall Tunnel used as a mortuary. Walking home from school at two o'clock one morning, passing holes in the road and seeing shattered fronts of buildings; I try to forget the silent figure I saw lying by one of these holes. Raids every night for three weeks—no sleep—a raid on Saturday morning at eleven o'clock in broad daylight—watching the ominous flight and the futile bursts of shrapnel.

No time of the day or night safe.

No sleep except in broken snatches.

Apprehension the whole time.

Lights in streets dimmed to maddening point; everything crouching.

Fear everywhere, disguised by hysterical courting in the darkened streets.

At the Alhambra—watching George Robey—the theatre almost empty while bombs and guns thud to the cracks of George.

Dark railway stations with wounded coming in, feebly happy to be home if only to die.

Christ! Christ! can one ever look at a young man again without wondering if he will live to grow old and cultured, or hear of a child being born without seeing it in a gas mask.

For the civilian the menace of the skies.

For the man on service: boredom, filth, horror.

On the sixteenth day of June 1918, at the age of eighteen, I received official papers telling me to report at Whitehall in a few days' time.

CHAPTER IV

INTERIM

June 1918—January 1919

'WE don't want to lose you, but we think you
ought to go.'

Words! Words! Words! In print, poster and
song. Droppings from the lips of beauty chorus and
suburban miss at the Sunday piano—words that nagged
at the youth of England month after month. The refrain
lilted cheerfully round corners and the wind carried it
into every home that might be hiding some strapping
youth too big for his years who 'really ought to join up,
you know'.

I set out for Whitehall with the sensation that everything was slipping away: all past efforts wasted; only
the horror of killing ahead.

At Great Scotland Yard (I never go past that street
now) queues of pale men. Line up there! Look sharp!

Hours slipping by doing nothing—looking sharp—at
nothing. The day passes—it takes one day to turn a man
into a sheep, though it has taken many years to make
him into a man.

The same evening—in barracks, getting into ill-fitting
uniforms that are crawling with animals (very small,
however). Two hours to go for a disconsolate walk—
do your buttons up, blast you!

Next day—gas chamber to kill the small animals, and
then on the train for camp somewhere in Staffordshire.

Crowds of soldiers everywhere—amazing that so
many men are left to kill off. All boys in our train—

E

already slipping away from civilization, cutting off window straps in an abandon of restraint and hiding their fear with reckless boasting.

Intensive training—lectures on disease, gas, in—out! on guard! shove it in 'is guts, it's not a tickling match! throwing bombs—stabbing—trailing imaginary guts on the end of a bayonet.

'Are you an artist? Can you draw me a naked woman?'

Four camps in one—British, Australian, W.A.A.C.'s and German (so clever to arrange for the needs of soldiers while keeping the enemy near at hand to goad them on)—the four horizons sore with huts and latrines. Huge parade grounds covered with large stones—two men and a bath collecting them shed a bitter tear.

'Blast this war!' says one of them. 'I'm only half English, anyway.'

Lights out: *enter the hut corporal very drunk, switches on the light, gets on table and tries to light cigarette from bulb. The boys chuckle obediently and the corporal looks round fiercely.*

Corporal: 'Funny is it? I'll make you bleeders laugh!' (*Gets off table and fixes bayonet. Approaching the end bed he points it at the boy's head in the perfect on-guard position. He was a very smart soldier.*)

Corporal: 'I'll show you how I killed Germans—the whole bloody lot of you!'

Bayonet crashes into wall of hut. Fortunately the boy ducks in time. Corporal walks round, stopping at each bed remembering details of everybody's ancestry, eventually falling on his bed weeping hysterically and killing imaginary Germans.

Killing—killing—killing: there is no end to dreams, and there's the rub. The great thing is to get through somehow—to come out the other end, as through a long, suffocating tunnel.

Something in being a mess-hut orderly—one could finish up the crusts of bread left over and, if lucky, scrounge a whole slice to eat in the lavatory. If only there were no washing up—hundreds of dishes in inches of greasy slime—not enough hot water—one's hands coated in disgusting muck like thick gloves.

On the parade ground: officers inspecting; our squad, every squad, acres of ground covered with squads making patterns as they drill, like blinded, agonized animals. Our sergeant sees a group of officers approaching. 'Now then,' says he, 'remember you're B Company.' Pride and love for his men came out in that remark (he was actually fond of us), we knew it and stiffened accordingly. Damn fools, but we were fond of him and couldn't help supporting him.

Phosgene Joe, with hardly any inside, tells us, with what is left of his voice, that bloody mugs like us don't stand an earthly. We know that only too well, Joe!

Quiet evenings in the camp library, a small hut that seemed so many miles away—two soldiers and the librarian, a quiet, peaceful man—looking at Hugh Thompson's illustrations to *Highways and Byways of England* with a sickening feeling that one would never see them again.

Gas masks in heaps—pick 'em up and hope for the best. Communal masks, since our own are not yet served out, with sweat and dribble from four companies.

'Gas alert! On! Quick march! Double! Run, you bastards! . . . Halt! Remove gas masks.'

'Anybody feel any ill-effects from the masks?' asks a

young gentleman with tabs. Only retching and spitting—'carry on!'

Carry on . . . nothing matters any more. There is an extra dose of slaughter in France just now; no leave, carry on—on—on—on. Orders cancelled and leave given for four days.

Four days of unreality—how return to civilized life when it must end in four days?

Four days of London—a queer place full of officers one had to salute. I had not realized until then how many officers there were.

Back at the railway station, full of troops and troop trains, some going to the front. A burly veteran, weighed down with equipment, weeps drunkenly: 'I don't want to go back to that bloody hell, I don't want to go.' Relatives and friends persuade him on to the train.

Bedlam everywhere.

Fear gripping at the bowels of everybody.

More weeks of training. Then the unbelievable news that the enemy is collapsing—it can't be true—we were meant to be killed—unfair to hold out hope.

November 11th—the Armistice is signed—a few feeble cheers and a mug hung up outside the canteen—immediate orders to pack for new billets at Norwich—everyone cleaning up and packing, too dazed to believe—no demonstrations—anti-climax everywhere.

How can we come alive so soon?—we need time, but the air smells sweeter.

Arrive at Norwich by midnight—a few civilians looking on curiously—walk up and down looking for billets and get shoved at last into a house where two of us fall into a real bed.

And then weeks of boredom. Ah, God! how one can be bored — nothing to do now, since there is no one to kill.

Invented drills—invented fatigues—cleaning—cleaning anything, it doesn't matter what it is, as long as a soldier is given something to do.

Xmas leave—and, by a lucky chance, demobilized because of a broken scholarship and a job to go back to.

Back to Norwich to sign off, before the rest of the company have returned, to hear that they are going to Germany with the Army of Occupation. Thank God it's not for me! Carrying revolvers into kindly German families is not my idea of seeing the world.

On to the Crystal Palace and, for the day, in a crystal stupor. Then home, feeling dull and depressed.

Are we free? Is the war over? Too many doubts and uncertainties to believe anything—just anti-climax.

We waited so long for the slaughter and it never came.

CHAPTER V

DURING the next eight months I completed my apprenticeship at Balham and tried to pick things up where I had left them. One of our men returned to the studio, but he left again after a short while: there was very little work to do, and he was too restless to idle quietly.

I remember nothing of what I did during those months at the studio, except that I made the acquaintance of an old Frenchman who printed coloured metal engravings, and that I spent many Saturday afternoons at his workshop somewhere at the back of Liverpool Street Station. He had, at one time, employed four printers, but the war had taken them as it had taken our staff, and he now worked alone.

For a while I contemplated joining him when I was free of my apprenticeship. I was etching at the art school in the evening, and with very little pressure would have taken to metal engraving. I enjoyed the deserted City on Saturday afternoons, and the approach to his workshop, through some passages, up an old flight of stairs belonging to a dilapidated scent factory, was an intriguing beginning to a pleasant afternoon.

He printed large plates of subjects by Morland, Gainsborough and Reynolds, each print taking about an hour to make. He rubbed the black ink into the sunk lines, wiped the surface clean, and then rubbed the colours on the cleaned surface with small 'rag dolls', as he called them, which were shaped rather like a cone with a rounded base. He knew his originals so well that he no longer used a colour guide. The prints he made were exquisite of their kind. He was excitable and enthusiastic about the pictures he was printing, and I was stirred to find out more about this business of picture making, or 'art' as it is called, for much as I enjoyed watching him print, I felt I would get bored with printing other men's work and would prefer to make my own pictures.

I decided to apply for a day scholarship at an art school, which would, incidentally, solve the problem of what to do when my apprenticeship finished. As an ex-service man I was not eligible for an ordinary scholarship, but the inquiry elicited the information that I could be given a Government grant which would cover the same ground. I winked at the irony of receiving such a gift in the company of a number of hard-bitten warriors, and so, in September, I left Balham in high spirits and came to work in London. I abandoned all ideas of earning a living—yes! I have to admit that I forgot the grim necessity of earning money, and slipped into the business of drawing and painting as one takes to the pleasures of a warm bath.

In the first week I saw a student at work on a large composition for the Prix de Rome, and for a while I was obsessed with the idea of Rome, until I discovered that Rome did not coincide with my ideas of freedom or art. Nevertheless, something must have taken root, for I started a large mural painting. This, by working on it two days per week, took me two years to abandon.

During the next two years, while I made sketches and studies, two full-size cartoons, and finally the mural, I

discovered—though I did not solve them at the time—
the many problems in designing a decoration.

I also discovered how very little I had to say, for,
having decided to do a decoration—it had to be something big—I was left with the problem of subject. I
abandoned the idea of selecting a subject from the Bible
or Shakespeare, partly because of the difficulty of
costume, and partly because I could get no further than
visualizing the subject: my imagination did not get as
far as the putting down on to paper. I solved the problem
by taking a subject from the streets, and since the subject
was obviously a makeshift, I fear it suffered, like most
art school compositions, from lack of purpose. It took
me two years to discover this and abandon the wall in
despair.

Composition is a baffling problem: it is difficult to
know how to teach it. It is not only a question of relating
forms, though pure æsthetics, as such, is an essential part
of every picture. Composition is, in a way, the mood
and meaning of a picture—the psychological structure.
Since every picture means something different, and
every artist is an individual, this structure must alter and
respond to the individual problem, which means that
the artist has to find himself as a person before he can
realize his particular problems in design. There are, of
course, certain fundamental laws of balance and harmony that are so well known that it is pointless to
discuss them here. These laws pervade all picture making,
and when applied to set problems are useful; but how
do they stand in relation to the quality of imagination?
Imagination brooks no interference, or disappears
completely if there is such interference. Anatomy to the

draughtsman must become a sense rather than a conscious knowledge, and just so the laws of design have to
become subservient to the imagination, else how should
we get variety and personality in art?

Since we cannot expect the student to be a resolved
individual, he must approach design through the
working rules. I suppose I must have developed my
sense of pattern while I was working on the decoration,
for I was most dissatisfied with it at the finish, and I
believe my main concern originally was to make the
pattern satisfactory.

The business of pattern making, however, is only a
part of design. Attractive shapes do not always mean
very much—indeed, sometimes they can mean precious
little. Harmony of tone, colour, shape and line is not
always expressive. Disharmony is just as important in
its right place: so, in life, is happiness and unhappiness.
Though I may envy the artist who works contentedly
with his rules and methods, I have no use for him: his
work does not move me.

Perhaps I am wrong to demand of the artist that he
should give more than quiet pleasure and relaxation, but
I cannot help feeling that it is his job to see, and to
express, life in the round.

I discovered the value of tone in design some few
years later. I was always conscious of shapes and colour,
but the lack of a tone sense prevented me from getting
any real satisfaction from my work for a long time. I can
remember when I did make the supreme effort to study
the tonal problem in painting and design for a few years;
I painted some very dreary pictures as the result of
sacrificing colour to tone.

The study of tone should be part of the early discipline
of the student. No artist can afford to evade this discipline in draughtsmanship. Observation and sound construction are essential, however experimental an artist
may be: he must learn to draw simply and accurately,
to see shapes and register tones and observe the character
of the model. When the mind is stored and the eye
trained, the imagination will make its own selection and
use technical skill in its own way.

I remember the confidence with which I sat down to
make my first art school drawing of the pears, and my
ultimate satisfaction with the result. Nothing bothered
me then, for my problem was simply that of representation, and its achievement a question of care and time.

When I began drawing as a day student, my point of
view was still somewhat similar, though perhaps not
quite so confident: and then came those disturbing
words, creeping into the talk about drawing—form,
rhythm, lyrical, plastic, planes. Hell! Why not just
draw the model as one saw it, why not trust one's eyes?
Why start all this mental stuff and get all emotional and
worked up? I looked round and, as far as I could judge,
the students who glared most at the model were making
very messy and inaccurate drawings.

The fact is that I did not understand or react to
emotion in drawing: it remained for some time a form
of study to me, and not a method of expression. I tried
for a while to lash myself into a 'state of mind', but
returned to making a careful line in an effort to study
character of form.

There is a grave danger in giving the emotions too
free a rein without craft to control them. The act of

drawing can so easily become a form of mental abuse.

Drawing for the sake of drawing, with no purpose or control, with no thought but that of creation, can lead to madness. It can dazzle and bemuse until the tired mind gives way. The charming boy starts to smoke and swear. He stands on his head in the life room. He draws circles and pipes while he chuckles at the model. The sky goes black and the 'donkey' jumps.

'Why shouldn't I paint the sky black?'

I reply that 'there seems no reason why not, if you want to paint it black.'

'But it is black.'

Good God! If the sky *is* black, then, indeed, all is lost. It is sad that the search for light can bring blackness.

We draw what we see.

But what do we see?

I do not see what you see; and then we both see differently to-day from what we did yesterday. Then how can we say what drawing is? Rembrandt, Blake, Utamaro, Picasso—are they all good draughtsmen?

Well, well! And I started off so simply with a couple of pears and was so sure that I knew the right way to draw.

The child says 'I want to do a drawing', does the drawing and thinks no more about it.

The adult says 'I wish I could draw', because he has lost the ability to do something and think no more about it: he has become self-conscious.

The child's world is a curious world. Its curiosity leads it on to the next thing to the exclusion of the last.

The adult mind is more difficult to satisfy. The idea of perfection is in his mind, however faint, and his wider experience renders him less certain than the child, while disuse has made him doubt his control over paint or pencil; and so he can only wish to draw. Yet even the faintest wish to draw is proof that the liver is not completely sluggish.

From putting a line round a thought with childish inexperience to making a drawing of pears with no thought but that of recording and observing is the first long but necessary step in the business of learning to draw. And from drawing pears in this happy and untroubled state, to discovering the real meaning of drawing, occupies the rest of the artist's working life. The first two phases bring peace and content. After that peace of mind comes only in patches. The desire to say something personal, combined with the delicate adjustment of the craft of drawing, is a constantly recurring problem. I show two diagrams that explain to me the states of mind arising out of this problem of the adjustment of technique and perception.

It must first be understood that the artist is not born, like Minerva, fully armed. He has to learn his job by years of effort: technique, imagination and perception are faculties that have to be developed by training.

In the following diagram the hand represents the craft and the eye represents the mind.

We begin in the happy state of drawing pears with a mental vision well below the craft ability: result—a happy state of mind. Then the mind begins to work, assisted, no doubt, by the practice of the hand, and we reach station one, and for a while hand and eye work in unison. During this period the artist is conscious of a

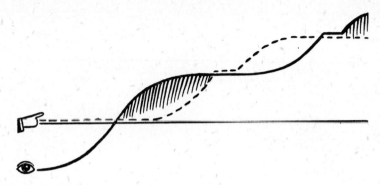

sense of power: he can draw and express himself with ease and fluency.

A point of departure is then reached. If the mind has been developing it leaps ahead beyond the artist's technical ability. The line showing this departure slows down owing to the drag of technical difficulties until the craft line comes up to meet it, makes a point of contact, and once more, for a while, the artist has synchronized his faculties.

The shaded portion indicates the period of time, well known to most artists, of despair and difficulty.

Thus we see how technique can, from being more than adequate, become useless. A new technique has to be developed by every artist for every phase of his mental progress. The more personal the vision, the more personal the craft must become. Progress ceases when the eye no longer stimulates the hand.

The next diagram shows the happy state of the man who starts off from the beginning by knowing what he wants. For a short period there is a perceptible struggle with the craft. The eye line is reached, and after a brief period of promising drawing the craft line soars ahead

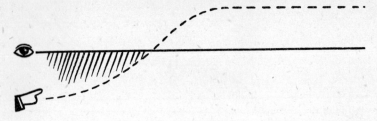

for a while, showing an increase of facility. The eye line, however, remains steady to its original purpose. Progress stops—facility is the more obvious quality and the mind remains for ever untroubled.

Blessed are the meek!

It is no wonder that parents discourage their children from taking up art, in spite of the legends that still exist of making a fortune. They suspect the worst and would prefer their offspring contented.

Perhaps the term 'relationships' best described the idea of drawing and composition. Forms placed in space achieve significance by the relationship of their true values. A line that moves into space without relationship to another line is a lost and meaningless mark.

Loneliness might be symbolized by a short line in infinite space.

The relationships of tone in nature must control the selection in a student's drawing for a while. The range of tone in nature is infinite, while the range possible with pencil and paper, and even paint, is limited. Selection is necessary in order to give a drawing clarity and intelligence.

Consciousness of function in form, and the effort to express it through constructive design, makes waste paper of the crammed notebooks on anatomy and perspective. Form can be made to exist independently of these physical and theoretical devices. Stress is not always shown by a bulging muscle, neither is space always conveyed by a correct vanishing point. Form, divorced from the idea of function, is seldom of any real value, and can only please the eye for a while.

By the time I had got to the stage of reacting emotionally through drawing in a genuine manner, I had begun to ask myself whether I had anything to say (a question that should occur periodically to every working artist).

It seemed unwise, and certainly dangerous, to go on indulging in emotional excess without reason; for, without reason, emotion can only float about in space like the unrelated line, and get lost.

I could decide to be a painter, I supposed, but that seemed rather risky—I was beginning to think of the need to earn a living. I consoled myself for a while by reasoning that painting would help me in whatever job I should do ultimately, and so, having eased my conscience, shelved the awkward question of application for a while.

I produced a painting that was accepted by the London Group (then showing at Heal's) and have called myself a painter ever since.

The same problem, however, arose in painting: had one anything to say as a painter? It was not good enough to paint for the love of painting and the handling of colour. Such easily won pleasure must surely be suspect, a Puritan outlook, I have no doubt, but I have long suspected the artist of being a Puritan. I discovered that other students had solved the problem more easily.

Those who were passionately interested in people expressed their sympathy by painting portraits or compositions from everyday life. Those intending to be commercial artists limited themselves to the newspapers or hoardings, while others contented themselves with allegory. When I had spent the first two years in an effort to finish one mural, I decided to experiment with a few crafts, hoping to find one that might be useful as a future source of income.

I had one year of security left, with no prospects beyond, and a periodic chill accompanied this thought.

I realized that the old masters had had their problems solved for them: religion, even if they were not religious themselves, had supplied the motive for most of their paintings. Safely tied down to their subject, they had poured themselves into a limited space and swelled it in proportion to their greatness. In them I discovered the art of illustration. They told a story in the picture, without fearing the loss of artistic integrity.

It must be remembered that in the years previous to and just after the War, English painters were obsessed with the problems of significant form. Such words as graphic, literary, sentiment, and so on, were the most damning remarks that could be made about a painting. I have no doubt that the attitude was a healthy reaction to the trite paintings that have filled our public galleries, but it checked the natural feelings of painters for many years, while they struggled to produce paintings that could not be recognized as any known arrangement of forms in nature, for fear that a motive, or story, might be discovered by some scornful critic. The natural result of this attitude to picture making was for the artists to turn away from illustration, for the first time in the history of art. Apart from portraits and landscapes the only recognizable objects that were permitted in painting were apples (fruit of every description, but mainly apples), violins, match boxes and frying pans, while the spaces between were filled up with draperies.

And so my interest in painting could hardly be expected to lead me on to illustration, an art that was suffering badly from the desertion of the artists and only maintained by a few discerning men who were then working in comparative obscurity as far as I was concerned.

The study of the old masters corrected this influence to a certain extent, and enabled me to hold on to my affection for Cruikshank and Hogarth. I saw that the old masters were drawing for a purpose and bending their forms to express an idea—bending and twisting them until they cried out in anguish or settled down into infinite repose. I saw that each painter had resolved himself, and that he seldom bothered to go outside of his own vision—he was, in fact, expressing his point of view. The infinite variety, yet individually satisfying conceptions of the same motif, could only be accounted for by the sincerity of these painters and the courage they showed of their own convictions.

It is strange that with this discovery and an interest in illustrated books I did not take to illustration as a student. Perhaps I was doing so in my mind, for an undoubted interest was there, but in practice I did very little. I made one effort to illustrate some of Blake's poetic prose, which, needless to say, was an imitation of Blake. I designed wallpapers for a while, mostly to

F

develop my sense of design; a few months at this enabled me to appreciate shapes and textures as nothing else had done.

I tried lettering and discovered the difficulty of cutting a quill pen, and the beauty of the rustic capital and the half uncial. I had done plenty of lettering at the studio, but with no real knowledge of its forms: no doubt I had put thick strokes where there should have been thin. The trade marks and name blocks and slogans that I had invented depended for their commercial value on their difference from every other kind of letter: bastard is hardly the word for the letters I had quite enjoyed drawing. My interest in these bastard forms prevented me from becoming a purist, although I studied the construction of letters with as much interest as any medical student studies anatomy. I even introduced the rustic capital into a poster, and the awful moment came when I thought of illustrating a book and writing it in a half uncial of one of the best families.

This made me abandon writing—the illustrations were not even attempted; something was wrong!

I saw that the manuscripts in the Museum were good, and then realized that it was the date that was wrong: I had been trying to work in the Middle Ages and it had not suited me. I do not regret the effort, for in later years I grafted my knowledge of traditional letter forms on to my experience of lettering for commerce. When I had to design letters for book-jackets I found no difficulty in making a letter to suit the particular book.

I have heard it said that 'a letter is a letter', and talk of the a-ness of an A and the b-ness of a B. I find a letter more fluid than that. A letter in a page of manuscript is

one thing, and in a page of type it is another. It is often
a twig or an animal more than a letter: it is often so
much a part of a design that it ceases to have an independent existence. A letter is a symbol as fluid as any
of the forms in nature, and as capable of re-creation.

I went on to wood-engraving—an interest that was
partly fostered by the illustrations in old books that I
had found, and partly by the atmosphere that Noel
Rooke had created at the school, and outside it. He had
always been convinced of its possibilities as a creative
medium, although its long history showed it, with a
few exceptions, to be a means of reproducing a drawing
in multiple. In spite of opposition, he persisted in teaching what was looked upon as a dead craft, and, a pioneer
himself, he was convinced of its possibilities and probable revival in a different status. The modern wood-
engraver owes much to his efforts. There are few who
are not his students or students of his students. By visits
to the Museum, and long enthusiastic discussions, he
showed me how nobly the craft had supported book
work from the first days of printing.

And so I bought three tools:

> a graver
> a spitsticker
> and a round scorper.

With a piece of end-grain boxwood, 2 in. by 3 in., an
oil stone and a sandbag, I was sufficiently equipped to
start engraving.

In this purchase I made the acquaintance of T. N.
Lawrence, of Red Lion Passage, Fleet Street.

I was reminded once more of my many visits to block-makers and workshops that had interested me so much in the past. Fleet Street once more; through Red Lion Court and up the usual staircase of tiled walls and strange trades going on behind mysterious doors. At the top, to find a second-hand Albion Press outside a door labelled T. N. Lawrence. Inside: the usual small office with a counter, and the old familiar rumble of machinery nearby. Around the walls were compartments filled with blocks of every size, and in a case were the tools that were to transform these acres of wood into a lacy pattern as lovely as the tracery of bare trees and carved ceilings.

There is no vulgar service of counter hands here. T. N. Lawrence himself presides, and handles his blocks and tools with fitting affection, and completes the picture with his whimsical personality. From that day to this I have purchased my blocks from him. He is a reliable man and has never let me down, even when working under pressure. The first thing he gave me, with my tools, was a lesson in engraving, and I have no doubt everybody else gets one too. His knowledge of engraving is vicarious but varied, and I have always found it pays to listen to gossip about a craft, even if it be outside my needs for the moment.

One's own job has a habit of linking up in the long run, and I regret none of the time I have spent in watching a craftsman at his job.

No man can, or will, tell everything of his craft: it is not possible. Part of it is in the way he sits and thinks and breathes: it does not occur to him to describe these, for he takes them for granted. But watch a craftsman and see where his elbows are when he is working quickly, and where they are when he is going slow; whether his feet are tucked beneath him or well in front. See how near he is to the source of light, and how long a tool he is using. Does he hold the block high or low? Does he engrave certain lines slowly and other lines quickly? His bench is covered with tools and strange oddments. Every craftsman has his own collection of oddments. If you ask what that piece of card is for or that piece of wood, you will find that it is either a new tool or some other aid to the peculiar technique of that craftsman. Years of experience have probably resulted in the invention of an odd accessory that looks like so much rubbish to the casual eye.

These are the things that the craftsman does not always talk of, but they tell you more of the inner life of a craft than any textbook.

Just as we have to eat many apples to know the taste of apple, so we must discover a craft from many craftsmen. We tend to forget how many human beings we have seen in order to get used to the idea of the human face. We take the variety too much for granted: we are naturally lazy and do not concern ourselves overmuch with subtle differences; yet it is in these differences that invention lies. While the fundamental mould may remain the same, its surface is constantly redecorated. Just as a boot will take the character of the foot, so will a tool take the character of the hand (which, it must be remembered, is controlled by the mind) and become invested with the personality of the craftsman.

The same tool can be used by different craftsmen for different purposes. Observation of this varied handling

will give a fairly good valuation of the potentialities
of each individual tool.

For instance, Miss A. wears a hat to keep the rain off.
Miss B. wears a hat to look attractive. Miss C. wears a
hat because Miss B. does. Juniors D. and E. wear their
hats because they've got to, and G. just wears a hat.
A knowledge of hats includes an understanding of all
these motives.

As I mentioned earlier, I bought three tools and a
block. The block itself is a beautiful piece of craftsmanship with its perfect joins and polished surface. Only by
suppressing one's appreciation of wood is it possible
to destroy such a surface.

All engravers must make themselves block-conscious,
or it might be more correctly termed print-conscious.
This consciousness can be developed from the beginning

by taking a print from the virgin block. This will show the glory of a solid black.

The print has its own quality. The even distribution of ink has a depth and texture that is the result of the virgin kiss of paper and block. No original drawing has this direct appeal of quality, and this must be understood by the engraver if he is to make an engraving and not imitate a drawing.

For my first block, lacking a suitable subject, I engraved a self-portrait direct from the looking-glass on to the block—I have never tried anything quite so courageous since. I had made no experiments with the

tool and had no idea of textures or tones. I made the engraving with one tool—the graver—and only used the scorper to cut away the background.

I have since evolved a method for beginners, based

on my lack of early experience, that incorporates knowledge of tool work and freedom of drawing. Although I lacked a knowledge of tool work, I did realize in my first block (though I lost sight of it immediately and for several years) that engraving could be a creative medium and need be no imitation of a drawing. The tool can be used as freely as a pencil. It took me a long time to recapture my first freedom, and I attribute this partly to my interest in the early books and their heavy woodcuts that stressed black line and contours.

I now feel it to be a mistake for any young engraver searching for technical inspiration to look at anything in the nature of a cut. A cut is essentially different from an engraving. Almost every black line engraving I have seen, that is working along the lines of the old cuts, is either a conscious effort to maintain the early *naïveté* and crudity, or has become sophisticated, suave and boring. I can remember engraving many blocks in some early books that were simple black lines, and for a while enjoying their simplicity and clarity; but the moment came when I realized that my increasing skill, resulting from practice, was destroying the pleasing irregularities that give the old cuts their quality. I was faced with the problem of submitting to enforced added efficiency (for I found it impossible to keep tool work unskilled, neither had I any convictions against such skill) or abandoning the black line for the more natural white line that the graver produces. It is now obvious to me that the student must start from Bewick and go on through the nineteenth century, even up to the decadence of engraving, and make use of the whole of the last two centuries of engraving in order to give his work a contemporary flavour and to exploit the medium to its fullest extent.

I used the graver in my first four blocks, and only then, to suggest tones. It is true that I tried to get these tones simply, and without cross-hatching, by exploiting the direction of lines to suggest planes, but the idea of textures never entered my mind. This may have developed my sense of tone in engraving: it may be the reason why I still use the graver more than any other tool; I still do not rely on textures to explain drawing.

The shape of the graver should be

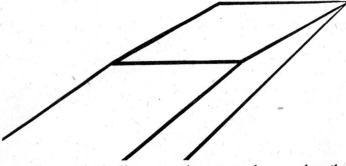

This allows the tool to pass over a large block and, at the same time, maintain the correct horizontal position. Any lift off the horizontal will cause the tool to bury and bring the line to a stop. This also applies to the spitsticker.

The graver has an insinuating point

Its shape, which allows it to bury into the wood easily, enables it to pass rapidly from a hair line to a wide line by a slight lift of the handle. It will take a curve at a swinging pace and produce a delicate even line if the point is kept up on the surface in a kind of floating movement. It will clear a sharp angle at one stroke, and pick a fine stipple with delicate precision. It will re-enter a fine line and, with a little pressure, swell out that line to give it a belly and then grade back to the fine line again with a lifting movement: the action might be called a scoop. This can be done on curved or straight lines.

The tool must be held in a position that is natural to the individual and his method of drawing. It is advisable to make an effort to hold the tool in one or other of the ways shown by the photographs, since there are excellent reasons for holding a tool correctly, but the final hold must be left for the engraver to discover for himself.

Underneath view of tool. Noel Rooke

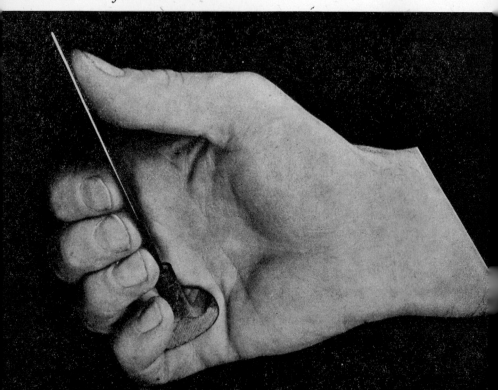

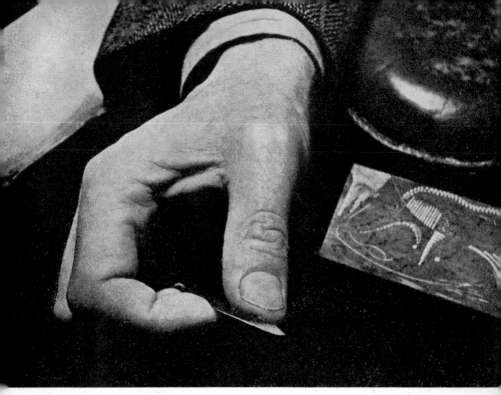

Front view of tool. Noel Rooke

Underneath view. John Beedham

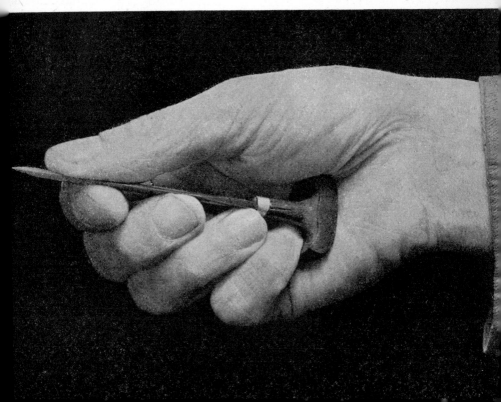

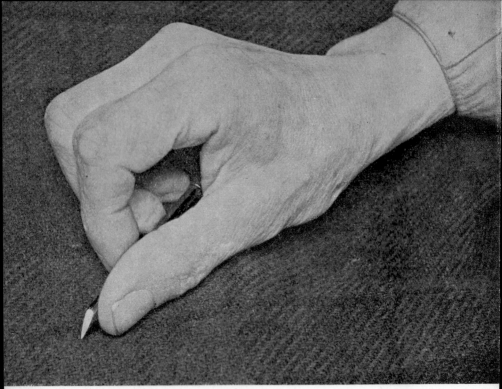

Front view. John Beedham

Underneath view. Gertrude Hermes

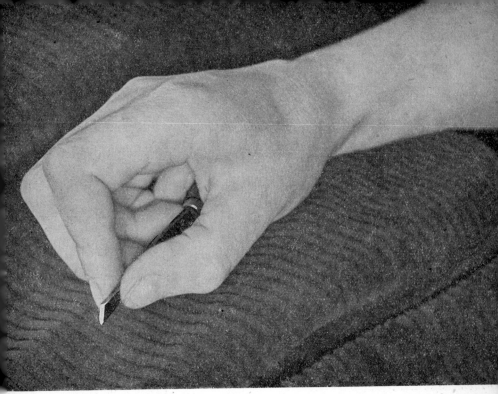

Front view. Gertrude Hermes

Underneath view. Ian Macnab

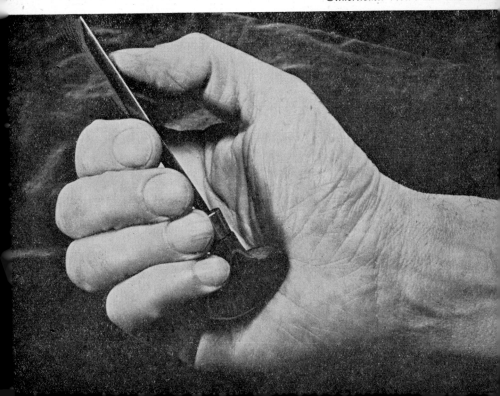

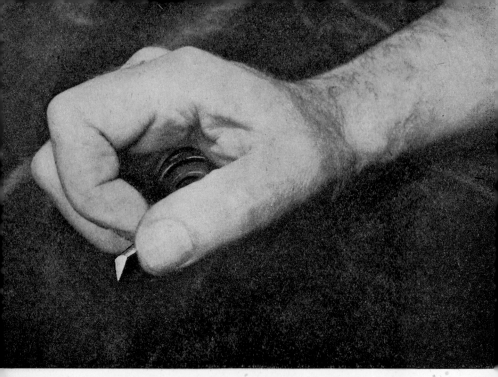

Front view. Ian Macnab

Underneath view. Blair Hughes-Stanton

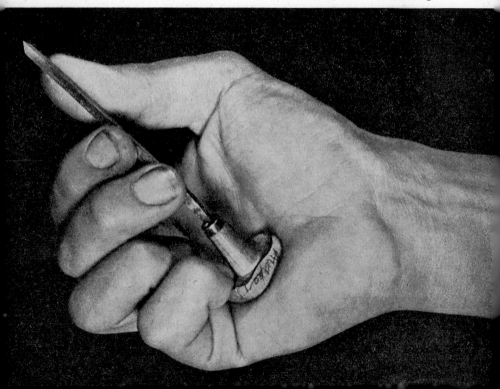

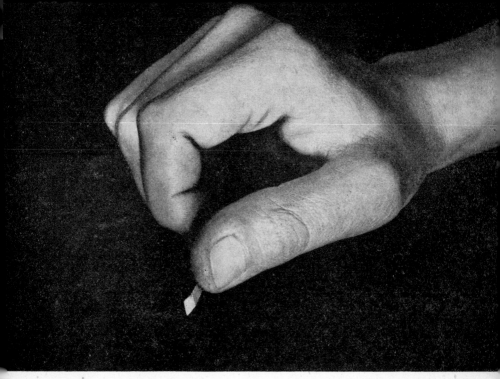

Front view. Blair Hughes-Stanton

Underneath view. Lynton Lamb

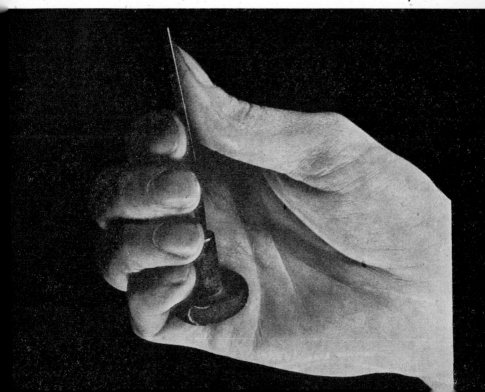

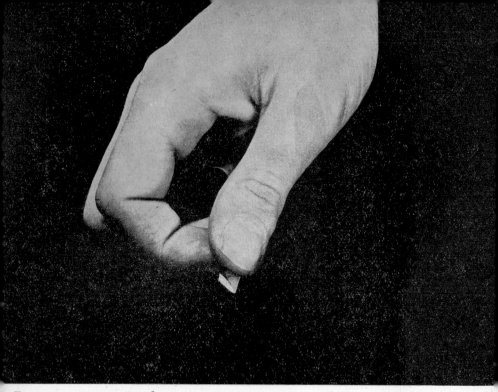

Front view. Lynton Lamb

Underneath view. Clifford Webb

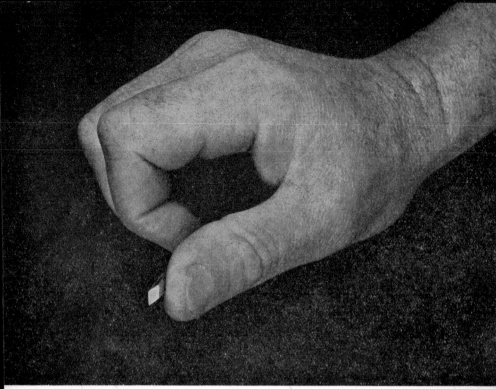

Front view. Clifford Webb

Underneath view. John Farleigh

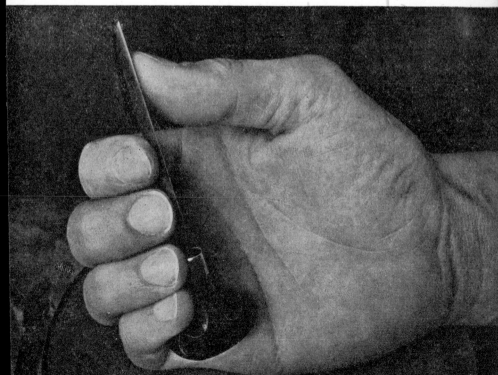

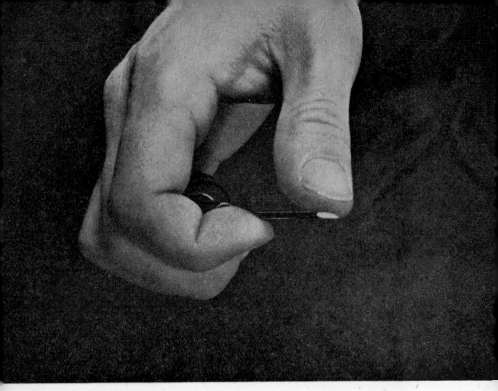

Front view. John Farleigh

These ways of holding the tool should be a starting-off point; the hold natural to the individual will follow in time. The length of the tool must be adjusted to the size of the hand and length of fingers: a short tool is always more useful than a long one.

HOW TO SHORTEN THE TOOL

Put the tool in a vice and tap off the handle with a hammer.

Tap the end from side to side gently, until it snaps off.

Raise the tool in the vice and file end to a point, shaping it at the opposite angle to the cutting point.

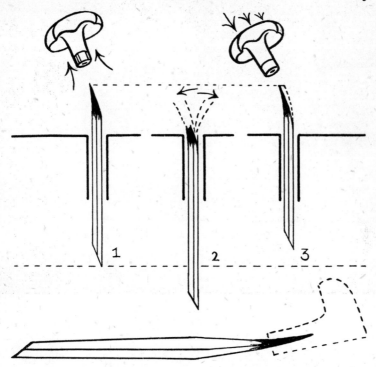

This ensures the handle going back at the correct angle.

Tap the handle back gently into position. If it is hit hard it will split.

A *sharp tool* is essential to good engraving and much safer to use. A blunt tool will jump the line and slip across the block and, owing to the extra pressure necessary to cut a line with a blunt tool, is liable to make a bad stab in the hand that is holding the block.

The tool should be tested at the beginning of each working day and at intervals throughout the day. Testing a tool becomes one of the automatic actions of the day's work.

To test for sharpness, hold the handle of the tool lightly in one hand and slide the point across the thumb-nail of the other hand, using little more pressure than the weight of the tool.

If it catches on the surface of the nail the tool is sharp enough. If it slides over the nail the tool is definitely blunt.

'Have you sharpened your tool lately?' I asked a bright young student.

'Oh no,' she said, 'it was sharp when I bought it.'

TO SHARPEN THE TOOL

Place the face of the tool flat on the oil stone and rub

gently in a circular movement. This applies to all the pointed tools.

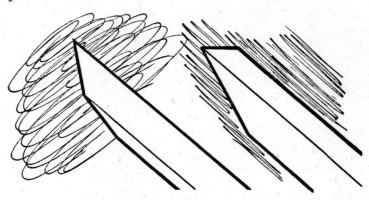

For flat-ended tools, like the square scorper, the movement is up and down. This saves the square corners from being rounded off.

The graver should now be sharp and of the right length.

The light should be coming from the opposite direction to the tool hand so that no shadows are cast on the block.

The back should not be bent too much or, as an old textbook tells us, 'The seed of chest disease is planted'.

I don't yet know if this is so, but I do know that if the block is too low it is very uncomfortable. If the sandbag is built up on some books the height can be properly adjusted and space will be left for the elbows to work free of the bench. A sandbag is necessary, as it gives the maximum stability combined with freedom of movement. As so much engraving depends on the mobility of the block itself, this point is an important one.

John Beedham

POSITION FOR WORKING

The photographs show the hand well below the surface
of the block; should the tool slip there will be no risk
of a stab, as the tool will pass over the hand. The wrist
has the maximum of flexibility in this position and can
control the turning of the block easily.

John Beedham

Noel Rooke

The contact of the tool hand with the block is shown in this photograph. The hand has been placed on an inked block and the contact has printed off on the hand.

The thumb is the main pivot and rests firmly on the block, care being taken that the nail is not too long, as it may scratch the surface.

The hands of Rooke, Beedham, Lamb, Macnab, and Stanton show the same impression. On the opposite page are the two exceptions. Gertrude Hermes's hand contacts on the wrist—all the fingers being quite clear of the block. Clifford Webb shows a contact with the thumb, the first three finger tips and knuckle of the little finger. It is an interesting comment on variety of handling, and shows, more clearly than the other photographs, the difference in technique.

John Farleigh

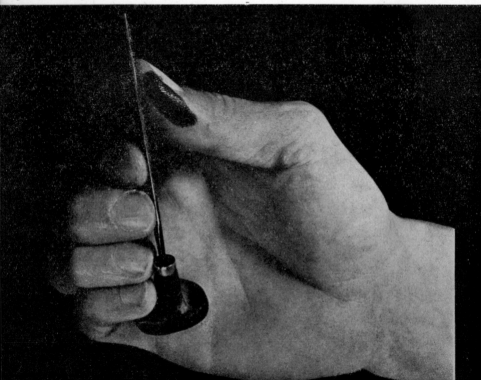

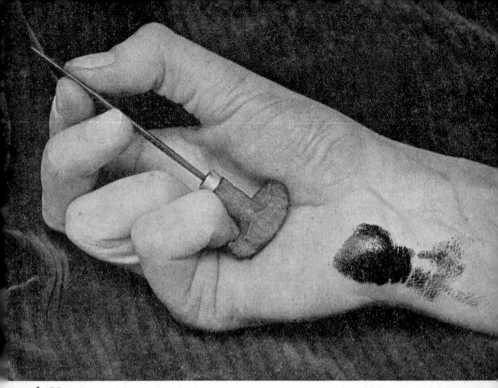

ertrude Hermes

Clifford Webb

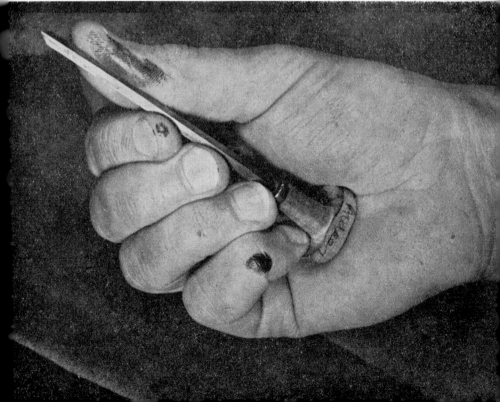

TO ENGRAVE STRAIGHT LINES

The tool slides along the ball of the thumb by contracting the hand; the average movement forward of the point of the tool being three-quarters of an inch while the thumb and the block remain stationary. To continue the stroke, the point of the tool remains at rest in the line while the thumb slides forward a sufficient distance for a repetition of the tool stroke. All beginners should take note that straight lines are engraved slowly and in short stages. Longer strokes are possible when considerable skill has been attained.

TO ENGRAVE CURVED LINES

To engrave *straight* lines the tool is driven into the block. To engrave *curved* lines the block is driven on to the point of the tool. The tool is held firmly against the thumb, which slides over the surface of the block as the curve is taken; but the maximum of movement is made by the hand holding the block. This hand should be twisting and turning the block on to the tool and controlling the curve at the same time. The tool hand can only move a little as it adjusts the accuracy of the curve. When making a short curve the thumb remains stationary and the tool moves along it a little as the block is turned on to the point. When taking a sharp curve the angle of the tool should be raised a little, or the line will be bruised by the heel of the tool.

Curved lines can be taken fairly quickly, unless you are trying to engrave a perfect circle, when it is necessary to guide the tool slowly, taking the complete circle in a series of short arcs.

TOOL WORK

The following description deals with the three tools mentioned so far: the graver, spitsticker, and round scorper.

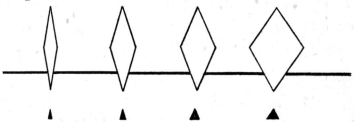

The Graver

The graver is shown end on as it cuts into the wood. It will be seen from the diagram that the width of the line is controlled by the depth of the tool. It is not advisable to force the tool too deep: this requires too great a physical effort, which destroys sensibility in drawing. A wider tool should be used, the range being fairly considerable from the narrow to the wide.

One stroke of the tool of three-quarters of an inch in length, that begins with the point up on the surface of the block and buries to- wards the end, produces

The shorter strokes achieve the same width as the long one by raising the handle of the tool, which buries the point more rapidly. This is useful when clearing an angle. The stroke should be finished by lifting the point upwards and slightly forward—almost a picking movement. This clears the wood at the wide end, which would otherwise project above the surface and make a faulty print. It will be seen that the white mark of the tool corresponds to its section.

The graver will also make an even fine line with comparative ease, but the tool must be kept fairly flat to counteract the tendency to bury.

The following is a short selection of tints and textures possible with the same tool, ranging from single tints to a combination of three, one on top of the other. It will be seen how easily this range can be extended.

1. Even fine tint, tool almost horizontal.

2. Same as No. 1, except that lines are packed closer.

3. Graded tint made by burying tool.

4. Long stipple tint with tool held at slightly higher angle than Nos. 1 and 2.

5. Short stipple tint with tool held at slightly higher angle than No. 4.

6. Fine graded stipple made by a picking movement with the tool held at a high angle.

7. No. 1 with half cross-hatching of similar tint in two different directions.

8. No. 2 with half cross-hatching of similar tint in two different directions.

9. No. 3 with cross-hatching of similar tint.

10. Top half, No. 4, interlocked with No. 1.
Lower half, cross-hatched with No. 2.

11. Nos. 4 and 5 interlocked (right half).

12. No. 6 with No. 3 superimposed in opposite directions.

13. Same as No. 11 with No. 4 super-imposed at angle on No. 5 (left half).

14. No. 9 with No. 5 superimposed.

To thicken a line as shown in diagram the line must be re-entered. An expert engraver can thicken a line as he goes by dipping the point of the graver and lifting it again to the level of the original, but even an expert must re-enter if any considerable thickening up is necessary.

To re-enter, drag the point of the tool lightly and backwards along the line where the thickening is to begin; this ensures the point getting into correct position in the line. Then scoop the tool downwards and up-wards, coming out again at the point where the line should regain its normal width. If necessary, repeat this action until the right thickness is obtained. It is better to make several strokes than to force the tool too deep, otherwise the line will get bruised.

The Spitsticker

This tool, like the graver, reveals its section in a down-ward stroke, and, again like the graver, it can make a line of even thickness by keeping to the surface of the block.

In both cases, however, the line will start with a point, as the heel of each tool is modelled to an edge

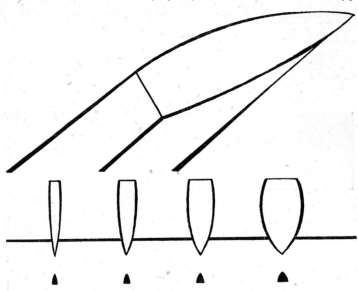

like the keel of a ship. Almost every remark made for the graver applies to the spitsticker. The only essential difference is the character of the line. The spitsticker makes a fatter line and thickens at a shorter distance from the starting point.

 When a careful comparison is made it will be seen that the shape of the cut is different also.

If the same exercises were made with this tool as those described for the graver, and the proofs were compared, the main difference would be seen in the general fattening up of lines and consequent lightening of tones. The difference of shape would be more noticeable in the stipples, where the dot is a different shape from that made by the graver.

The varying qualities of stipple to be got by using different shaped tools is worth studying.

A generalization might be made from the description of the two tools: the graver is used for the darker tones and the spitsticker for the lighter tones.

 Example: lay a tint on a small square with a graver; then continue those lines on to the next square with a spitsticker. In the second square the white lines will be thicker while the spaces between the lines will be thinner: result, a lighter tint.

The gradation obtained this way is rather sudden and useful for rapid changes of tone. The more subtle changes can be got with the graver alone, as already described.

The Round Scorper

This tool is generally known for its usefulness in clearing the waste wood from the block.

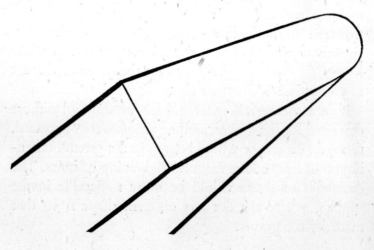

An excellent light tint can be got by packing lines close together.

If the same exercises as for the graver and spitsticker are tried with this tool it will be seen that its drawing capacity is more limited.

HOW TO CLEAR AWAY THE WOOD UP TO A FINE LINE WITH THE ROUND SCORPER

The photograph shows the scorper in position with a piece of card underneath the tool. This acts as a lever and protects the work at the same time, a protection that is highly necessary, for an excellent engraving can be ruined in this stage.

A narrow scorper should be used to clear up to the line, and a wider scorper to make the cleared space wider. The tool should not be forced to clear too much wood at a time, nor make too long a stroke. A number of short strokes will chew away the wood easily and without strain on the tool or the hand.

This block shows the progressive stages of clearing. The first few strokes are made away from the line, when the tool gradually feels its way up to the line; speed and caution are thus combined.

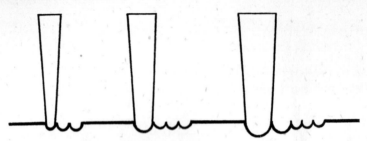

When all the lines have been cleared, the larger spaces of waste wood still left can be knocked away with a gouge and mallet, or the blockmaker can rout them out by machinery.

THE SQUARE SCORPER

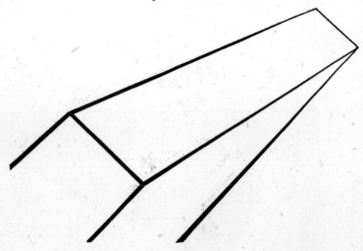

I found that this was the first that I added to my collection of three, when I did buy a new tool. Although it is possible to go quite a long way without it, I feel that the beginner would be wise to purchase it with the other tools.

Owing to its shape its function is very limited, but it does what no other tool can do.

It can clear a wide corner in two strokes and preserve the clean edges of the line perfectly. Owing to the flatness of its cutting edge the beginning of the stroke always prints badly; the shelving down of the cut, from the surface of the block, is too gradual to print clean.

This characteristic can be utilized when a gradation of tone is passing into a clear white.

The sloping edge left by the scorper helps the tint to fade off softly. I believe there is a way of sandpapering an edge down to get a similar effect, but I have never tried it.

The next diagram shows the square and round scorper in use for clearing purposes, and demonstrates their different functions. It will be seen quite clearly which tool is used.

SUGGESTIONS FOR FIRST THREE BLOCKS

I have evolved a method of teaching engraving which depends upon the execution of the following three blocks. I have proved, by results, that these exercises, while giving an opportunity to practise with the tool and to understand it, still leave plenty of room for the student to exploit his individuality. Each student who has made these experiments has produced a different effect.

The First Block

Approximate size of blocks, 2 in. by 3 in.

If there is time, the block should be given a thin coat of printing-ink and left to dry for a day or two; otherwise give it a *thin* coat of dark grey, made with process white and black. The dark ground will enable the cut to be seen clearly, though ultimately the engraver has to work by feel and knowledge of the print rather than by the appearance of the block.

Mark out the block into squares with a soft pencil and engrave the lines as shown in the next diagram, making every effort to keep the lines perfect and to start and stop at the right place.

Proof at each stage shown, and arrange the proofs consecutively on a page in order to see the development clearly.

1st stage

Use the graver and the spitsticker alternately to fill in the squares with tints, each square having a tint of a different width and direction.

2nd stage

Now commence to cross-hatch, varying the tints as in the last stage.

3rd stage

The student must now use his fancy for any further elaboration.

A third tint can be superimposed in certain places. If care is taken it will be possible to leave some of the first tints showing, the second and third, making a gradation towards a lighter tone. This will show the possibilities of texture combined with tone—the keynote of all engraving. The block should be engraved slowly and with an effort towards perfect tool work.

4th stage

When the third tint is superimposed it will be seen that the block consists of grey tones, most of the solid black being destroyed. These tones will be given a better value if a few pure whites are added (or taken away, as it is called, in engraving). The student's sense of design must dictate where and what the shapes of the whites should be.

The page of proofs should be carefully preserved, as it will provide a useful key for future reference.

The following blocks are made by beginners under the conditions described, and show the possibilities of variety though working to the same directions.

S. Fausset

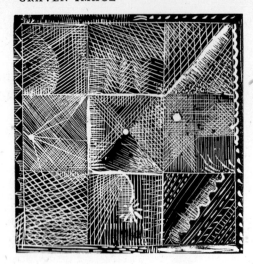

John Parsons

A. I. Lorimer

The Second Block

This block introduces the curved line and tint. Confidence is necessary—even if it is an effort—in order to carry this block through; perhaps abandon is a better word—the same kind of abandon that is essential in taking the first dive.

The tool should be placed in position and the block swung about in every direction, taking slow curves or quick corners, the tool hand moving and turning slightly in sympathy with the block. The result of this continuous twisting line can only be appreciated when the first proof is taken. The quicker the line is engraved the better it is likely to be.

1st state

John Parsons

The block is now divided into spaces of different shapes and sizes, unlike the regular division of the first block. These spaces will suggest a tone, tint or texture according to the fantasy of the student. From first to last the block is demanding the sensibility of an instinctive

designer. A few tints might be laid on and a proof
taken as soon as further progress becomes difficult.

A little white paint on the proof will enable the
engraver to decide any uncertain point in procedure.

3rd state

This can go on until the engraver feels that a satisfactory balance has been achieved.

Final state

Final state

A. I. Lorimer

Honor Frost

A. I. Lorimer

J. M. Sanders

Ann Hook

S. Silvey

Dorothy
Griffiths

The Third Block

The experience and confidence gained in the first two blocks must now be brought to bear in producing this block, which must start off with a subject of some sort, however vague.

Let us assume the subject is a figure and a tree. The graver once more wanders over the surface of the block, as in the last exercise, but there is now some effort to control the lines to express an image of a tree and a man. The shapes may not be clear at first: they will evolve in time. The final print may bear but the faintest resemblance to the original idea, but, nevertheless, the student has made a great step: he is creating an engraving. The first two blocks will make this easier than it sounds.

1st state

John Parsons

Final state

George Downs

Mary Farleigh, age 8 years. Simple white line design on black.

Age 8 years. Introduction of texture.

Age 8 years.

*Age 9 years.
Development
of tone sense;
result, black on
white design
instead of white
on black.*

*Age 9 years.
Experiment
in textures.*

*Age 9 years, showing more
control over tool work and tone.*

The student is now ready to engrave from drawings, and the questions arise: 'What sort of drawings?' and 'How are they transferred to the block?'

To the first question there is no answer. Any sort of drawing, as long as it conveys an idea, is capable of being translated into engraving. It might be remembered, however, that if a drawing resembles the wood-engraving too closely it is less capable of interpretation; there will be a tendency to imitate the drawing when engraving, just as there was a tendency to imitate the engraving when drawing. A free pen-and-wash drawing leaves more work for the tool to do at the moment of cutting, and this forces it to greater inventiveness.

A drawing may be made direct on the block in:

> pencil
> brush
> pen-and-wash

The block must be prepared with a very thin coat of process white for any of these media to take on the wood.

Advantage: all preliminary drawings and labour of transferring same removed.

Disadvantage: progressive proofs cannot be taken without risk of destroying original drawing before the engraving is finished.

TO TRANSFER A DRAWING TO THE BLOCK

Make a simple tracing of the main shapes and contours.

1. Rub down with a burnisher on to a block prepared with white and engrave almost direct from original, or

2. Trace on to inked block with red carbon paper.

Advantage of (1): further drawing can be added if

desired, and tones laid on with wash or pencil. Advantage of (2): the black surface shows up work clearly as the graver cuts down into the lighter coloured wood.

The only conclusion that can be drawn from studying these different methods is that preparation and approach must be adjusted to every different problem.

If a bad mistake is made the block can be resurfaced by Lawrence at half the cost of a new block. If the mistake is a small one the block can be plugged. In all emergencies I send the block to Lawrence—he is the G.P. for all ailments relating to the wood block.

If the student has followed engraving up to this point, he should be able to go on for some time without further assistance, since everything now depends on his ability to draw and his application to the craft.

I have described engraving for the student, not as I learnt it, but as I have since learnt to teach it. I did not apply myself to engraving for some years, and only discovered the technique very laboriously. If I have inserted so much detail at this stage, it is because I feel the student should learn to use tools as soon as possible, and not wait, as I did, for chance to put some work in his way before getting down to the professional side of engraving.

My interest in engraving faded out after the second block, which was an effort to use a life drawing in an allegorical design.

I have forgotten the third block, which indicates that it was a hopeless failure, and I did no more engraving for two years.

I went on to posters, for the L.C.C., in a moment of enlightenment, had commissioned the school to make

I

a series advertising the trams. Everybody was busy doing posters and, for a while, pen-lettering flooded the hoardings.

The weeks passed by quickly and the necessity for thinking of a job became unpleasantly obvious. I considered my qualifications and laid them out in order. I had been black-and-white artist, wax-engraver, photographer, machine minder, errand boy, letterer. I had tried etching, lithography, wood-engraving, posters, book illustration, wallpaper design, mural decoration, landscape painting, and made one design for the theatre. I was an expert at nothing, except, perhaps, wax-engraving, but I had no desire to return to this, even if a job could be found.

While I was realizing, in a bitter moment, that I was no more than an amateur, I was asked to design a window bill for a firm that made toffees. 'Would I make a drawing of some attractive children enjoying sweets?' Thank God I failed! With grim determination I decided to enjoy my last few days of drawing from a model.

At the last moment a teaching post fell vacant at Rugby and I was offered the chance of applying for the job. Teaching was the one job I had never contemplated, but since knowing a little of everything seemed to be a qualification for the sort of work I would be expected to do there, I swallowed my dread of talking in public in my relief at the possibility of getting a job of any kind. Besides, I was only expected to work some fourteen hours a week, and I should have plenty of time to go on dabbling in the way that had become so attractive.

Research is a seductive occupation, but it has its drawbacks. If only one could be content with achieving

enough skill to do one job well! If only ideas would not
flow through the mind, leading one on like a will-o'-
the-wisp! But one medium, by its very limitations, will
suggest what could be done with another, and a different
medium will express a different facet of the imagination.
I have turned a wash drawing or a water-colour into an
oil and then into an engraving, and each time a different
aspect of the same subject has been revealed. After the
close work of engraving I have turned with relief to the
fluid and ephemeral quality of a water-colour and then
returned with pleasure to the more exacting demands
of wood or metal.

It is in the nature of man to need change and relaxation,
and I bear in mind the awful stories of the specialists who
draw shoes or hats for a living until they can see and
think of nothing else.

How should one advise the student—to specialize
early and make sure of a job, or experiment and run the
risk of unemployment? Life is not worth living if a few
risks are not taken, but it is easier to take risks oneself
than advise others to do so.

I interviewed Vaughan, who was the headmaster at
Rugby. He seemed bewildered by the amount and
variety of work I had taken, but I was duly appointed.
I then settled down to enjoy what I had imagined to be
my last long summer vacation in preparation for the
ordeal in the provinces that was to begin in the following
September.

CHAPTER VI

THE PROVINCES, 1922–1924

THE wrench of leaving London and all its associations was softened by the security of a permanent job. I had had no previous experience of a provincial town; after making some effort in the train to visualize the future, I gave myself up completely to whatever lay ahead.

On my arrival I dumped my belongings in my room and walked round the town, knowing that it would be the only time that I should be able to do so without being recognized and saluted by the boys who were sauntering around. I was a stranger for one day only, knowing nobody and dissociated from every human contact, taking no part in life, yet left free to absorb. It is a similar condition to that of the artist in a fallow period: receptive, but not giving; a passive, empty vessel, filling up slowly until absorption point produces an overflow. It is necessary for the artist to be an empty vessel at times, however unpleasant it may be. The layman who thinks the artist has an instrument in him that plays at will is sadly wrong. I have been told that an artist should not be paid for his work, because he appears to be enjoying himself. If any man thinks that, let him go into solitary confinement for a while where there is nothing left him but to think: he will then begin to understand the mental difficulties of the artist who is always asking himself, 'What shall I do? What shall I say? How shall I say it? Is it important?' Then he will cry aloud for mercy and ask God to stop his mind from working, and give him quiet.

He will creep back to his rut and be thankful if he is still unable to see over the top of its ridges. It is not advisable to try the experiment, for a return to the rut is not always possible. Such a traveller into the forbidding spaces of thought may only avoid brain fever with the help of Hobbies Ltd. Many souls have been saved by a fretsaw or a hand-made whistle; while having no use for the amateur myself, I realize that he is saving his soul in his own way, and is therefore justified. Myself, as an empty vessel, on this first day at Rugby, registered an uninteresting main street, a few meagre suburbs, a host of careless, rather grubby boys, and some ghostly citizens— ghostly because they were not yet in focus to me.

I returned to my lodgings for my first meal. My landlady had a large goitre.

Later that evening I received a visitor who apologized for intruding, introduced himself as the head of the local art school, and asked me to supper the following evening, which was Sunday. For the next two years I was to spend every Sunday evening with him—evenings that were filled with discussions on every possible subject. He had an extensive and varied collection of books, and I left each Sunday laden with reading matter.

During the week I would retire peacefully with Landor's *Imaginary Conversations* or creep up to bed after reading Jung's *Explanation of Hallucinations,* with a wary eye on the shadows from my candle and anxious glances at the partly-opened doors on the landings.

'There is nothing either good or bad, but thinking makes it so', and we are lonely creatures in the world of our thoughts. If we could only understand and use that loneliness, we should be masters of ourselves. To trust our own vision, and to have the courage of our thoughts, is surely ninety per cent of creation. The smoke of civilization tends to blur the clear windows of the mind, and it certainly seems safer to keep those windows dimmed when one's neighbours' are dirty. Men have been crucified for having too clear a vision. Perhaps the real difficulty is in believing that our own point of view is sufficiently important to justify the effort of spring-cleaning, yet sincerity is the only way of producing original work.

Landor and Jung—Pater and Lewis Carroll—Blake and Hogarth—all had their own visions, and the varied images they have created fill our minds at the mention of their names. These images that the artists have made for us go to make up part of the pattern of life that is called experience, and are not to be ignored.

The name Rugby conjures up memories of those Sunday nights and working at the art school, which I was allowed to use as a studio.

And what of teaching small boys *art* at a public school? I had formed vague ideas of how I would teach, but I rapidly revised them. I learnt that the simple, apparently elementary things were the most important, and I am not so sure but what this does not hold good for everything. I must have mystified many small boys when I first started if, indeed, they ever took any notice of what I said. It is true that I had to work against the natural disadvantages of being next door to the tuckshop. I did not revise my ideas on small boys. I confirmed my suspicions that they were noisy, smelly, irritating,

sometimes unpleasant, sometimes very charming little
animals—in fact, much like small versions of grown-ups.
The mature man was delicately engraved on every small
face; a faint image that only needed time to put in the
light and shade.

I escaped, whenever possible, to the art school, and
continued to draw and paint, for I found it very difficult
to cure myself of the feeling, so easily fostered by art
school training, that unless I was drawing every day I
should forget how to do it.

I have since realized that it is essential to forget how
to do it before one can move a step farther, but I had
not then learnt how to use drawing as a means of
expression. It was still a form of study and, as such,
needed to be taken in regular doses.

There is something wrong in the student who leaves
an art school only to find he is still a student. The knowledge of himself and the ability to express that self
should begin to be manifest in his last year, or he is in
for a long season of drought—as, indeed, I was.

Since I had nothing to say, or perhaps no ability to
say it, I had no other course than to continue as a student
in my spare time, and exploit such opportunities as the
local art school offered.

I made copper bowls and bent metal into shapes,
which was a useful way of relieving my desire to beat
small boys.

I became enthusiastic over anatomy for the first time,
and worked with some of Leonardo's anatomical
drawings at my elbow.

I explored the regions of perspective until I succeeded
in drawing an icosadodecahedron in a given position

with its shadow and reflection thrown on a polished surface. I was saved from further effort by realizing that, apart from the actual thrill of making drawings of geometric forms in space, it was enough for the general purposes of the artist to know the eye level, and even that seemed necessary only on certain occasions.

I have since discovered that many artists have realized this fact in time to save themselves much labour and confusion of thought.

Since no form of study is quite wasted, however, for we extract experience of some sort in our own way from everything, I got something from the study of perspective apart from vanishing points and eye levels. I found an almost mystic quality in the placing of solid forms in space, and a sense of space and recession that is essential to an understanding of plastic design.

We are told to 'get things into perspective'; there must be something in it. We have to find our own position in space and time somehow, and the man who knows his vanishing point is certainly blessed. My fellow lodger was a drunkard and went a-whoring, but he was quite happy. Perhaps he had got things into perspective for himself.

So many long tables were needed for my last essay in perspective that I reached a stage when it became advisable to finish my drawing before going home, and I worked on into the small hours in the empty school, until a dead leaf, sliding down the roof, scared me into a fear of the cast shadows around me. Diagram and reality became badly mixed and I hurried out of the building, seeing spaces that receded into distant points that I could never reach.

So often in life we fix on a point ahead and try to reach it, only to discover that we have been running between parallel lines that can only meet in theory. Perspective can be summed up in the word 'illusion'. I have never consciously applied my knowledge of anatomy or perspective, but it developed my sense of construction and form as nothing else has done. This is to admit the wisdom of the traditional methods of training the art student, though I make the reservation that I did these things of my own free will. It is not every student whose senses need to be quickened in this way, and coercion can only engender distaste or boredom.

While I was making experiments and trying new crafts I was discovering a taste for music, and, in this, the school gave me plenty of opportunity, as music was, and probably is, a very strong part of the education there. I have forgiven many small pests for their Philistine behaviour in the drawing class after hearing them play a 'cello solo or conduct an orchestra.

And so, for two years, I continued to experiment with no particular leaning in any one direction. Perhaps I was taking teaching more seriously than I thought at the time, and it was absorbing most of my creative energy. I certainly overcame an almost morbid fear of talking in public by giving a lecture each term in place of a lesson. This meant lecturing thirteen times during the week, and the first week's efforts more or less blistered me through the awful sensation of stage fright. I suspect I learnt more by preparing the lectures than the boys did by listening to them.

Towards the end of my second year I took steps to return to London. The only job I was fitted to step straight into was teaching, for I could, at least, point to something done in that direction. Up to date I had not a single specimen that I could show to a prospective client that would convince him of my ability to carry out a job—apart from the posters I had made for the tramways, and posters are of little use as specimens for beginners.

I had allowed another two years to slip by without deciding to specialize, and in which I had indulged a passion for trying out new crafts and odd experiments.

I find this desire to experiment persists and is a thing I would like to discourage in all students if I could find it possible to lose that interest myself. Experiment is not the way to success. I would like to say to the student who has done a good job, 'Stop! Do nothing different from now on, but perfect what you are doing.'

Success lies in the repetition of a successful job, with the increasing efficiency resulting from such repetition. The client who gives the artist a job likes to feel that he is going to get the article he expects—doesn't every purchaser ask for similar assurance?

I show my latest book to somebody and a deep sigh is followed by the remark: 'I shall never like anything you do as much as the Black Girl.'

A press reporter writes: 'Are we to remember Mr. Farleigh only by the Black Girl?' when he reviews the book that I feel is my best effort so far. If I had been able to marry her I could have produced many more black girls and so lived successfully ever after.

But I can only say, 'To Hell with the job that is done!', and I would say 'To Hell with the student who refuses to experiment!' Students and artists must make their own choice—the soporific sedateness of success or the exhilaration of experiment. There is not much choice usually— you either must experiment or you can't—but I have no doubt I shall continue to urge the idea of experiment out of horror for repetition, even to the student that draws a dogged line from the first.

In parenthesis, I should like to add that, by experiment I do not mean that a man should learn to draw, to fly, to grow asparagus, to study astronomy and be a politician all in one brief lifetime. I am assuming a specialist point of view and thinking of it as the kingdom within a nutshell—a small space which can be expanded into infinity. To write this book is an experiment so far as I am concerned, and is useful to me, since it is related to my job and is clarifying my ideas while suggesting others; I would not dream of writing a novel, which is the job of a writer.

I suspect I protest so much because I envy the placid existence of the man who knows his limitations and accepts them. The dull man is not aware of his dullness and is therefore content, and who does not envy the contented at times?

I was not content teaching art in a public school. If I had to go on teaching it must be adults, or at least students, who intended taking up art seriously. London was essential to me for many other reasons and its atmosphere was necessary for any further development on my part. If I remained teaching small boys I must become a small boy myself. I'm afraid I had lost the taste for boiled sweets.

And so I returned to teach antique and still life at the Central School of Arts and Crafts.

'*Zoe*'

I spent my last afternoon at Rugby in the art school,
and to fill in time made my fourth engraving. I had
carried a spare block with me and the tools. A drawing
of a small negress suggested an engraving that would
be finished in the two hours I had to spare. The tones
were picked out with the graver—I did not think about

the technique of engraving. The block was hurriedly packed to be printed in London.

And this (shades of Tristram Shandy) brings us to the incident at the beginning of the book, and I can now proceed to develop the idea of illustrating and engraving, hoping that some ideas have been thrown out already, if only by the way.

CHAPTER VII

PRIVATE PRESSES

I RETURNED to London!

London is a wonderful heap of rubbish full of gems for those who will trouble to find them. I walked round, looking at its streets, knowing that every one contained some gem, even if at times that gem was well hidden. Only those who have known the paucity of atmosphere in a small provincial town can appreciate the generosity of London: yet even London will remain mute and shroud itself from the careless eye of the tourist-minded. To insist on reaching an objective ahead is to miss everything by the way. Reality is so often lost for the sake of a mirage, and to measure experience by a speedometer is to shorten our lives by just so many miles.

We start from a village in the morning, reach the end of the street by midday, and what have we seen? Some cabbages like great green blossoms against the brown earth; a puppy; a thistle six feet high. And talked to the man who is trimming the churchyard; hearing more local history than can be found in any book. And seen the labourer cutting a rick into great wads like tobacco, and in the evening sat on a warm brick wall and listened to the sounds of the earth, murmuring and thrusting through the pulsing light. The sun has wheeled across the sky and its arc is a measure of our fullness.

With hobnails it is possible to get round the National Gallery quite quickly. In the Victoria and Albert Museum it is advisable to go slowly or we may get lost.

As a student I once stumbled on a second-hand book shop; hardly a book shop, for it was derelict and dirty, while an enormous pile of books lay in the middle of the floor marked at 1d. and 2d. each, according to size.

Strange lonely figures bending over the books: objective, intense, searching; for what? an old treatise? an old textbook? a title-page? old illustrations? an old endpaper? rare bindings? Anything and everything is good to the insatiable appetite of the book-lover. If it is not food for the moment, it may be food for the future, while a whisper from the past is cherished as the firm voice of a contemporary.

The dirty shop and the noise of London traffic faded as I found myself looking at these books, and wondering why some of them were published, and what purpose they could have served. Then, speculating on the people who had bought them, what they were like, how they were dressed. A book has its own background; the inscription tells us so much of its owner.

Junk, and for the most part bad junk, yet they held me spellbound; dreaming of strange men and women, and of the queer toil of scholarship.

I picked up a book. It was filled with lovely copper engravings of flowers, interleaved with superb titles. It was exquisite! It was twopence! I hurried out, followed by a cursing fellow student who had been waiting for me to put it down.

In my hurry I forgot the position of the shop and could not find it again. If I had not the book to this day as a very treasured possession I should think it was a dream.

Every collector can tell of at least one experience that is a treasured memory.

Every day can show at least one important moment. Every visit to a museum will result in at least one important discovery.

If we go to a museum with an object in view, then we must be prepared to abandon that objective immediately, or the window of our mind is shuttered. Sunday afternoons, year after year, spent in wandering round a museum in which one was always lost. Lost also in the quiet happiness that is found in the beauty of simple things.

There is a great sadness in beauty. It pervades all museums and can be kept at bay only in the confidences of a close friend: a friend in a museum is necessary. There was so much beauty in all the small things of life at one time. Is man's unhappiness caused by the loss of this beauty, or has it been lost because of his unhappiness? The small things in life are so important. Icarus was a fool!

We cannot blame the machines entirely. They have always existed in some form, however simple; and it is proved that in proper hands the machine can do good work. It is love that is gone—love of wood and iron, and love of people—respect and friendship are now among the rareties. It is useless to hurry, thinking to catch up, for that is to pass everything by. We must loiter—be still—and wait. Stop the wireless!—stop the guns!—and listen! Love is close to the ground: in the grasses and in the sound of the wind. It is in a piece of china, or a fragment of carved wood. It is a quiet voice that cannot be heard without the effort of listening.

Coming from the museum a nostalgia descends for the beauty that was so hardly won and is so easily lost.

By their works ye shall know them—perhaps it is better to judge mankind in the museum than in the crowded Tube or from the headlines of the newspapers.

To-day, 22nd November 1937, I went to the Book Fair at Dorland Hall, and to-night I remember so little of what I saw. When I go round museums I never bother to remember names or dates: the personality of beautiful things is more important to me, and always has been. It gives something more valuable than knowledge. To know an artist's name does not imply an understanding of his work.

I saw so many books to-day—so many thousands— it would have been futile to try to remember them. But the sensation of books remains, their friendliness and feel, the dignity of a craft, even in a world where success is measured by the balance sheet. These things remain, filling me with a desire to make a book beautiful—to make something that will drop into place among the small things of life and to pass on something of the dignity and pleasure of a craft.

I loved books long before I helped to make them— from the day that I first read the *Four Georges* and discovered the beauty of words.

The love of words and sentences, of letter-forms, of a page of type, and the quality of the paper and binding, is a sequence of appreciation, and they followed one another slowly as I browsed among the book shops and museums. A desire was growing in my mind, to illustrate a book with engravings. I understood engravings in relation to book work more than the mechanical processes, because I never looked at modern books: I

K

confined my interests to the 1d. and 2d. boxes, expensive
antiques or the equally unattainable in the museums.

I had no sense of contemporary books—after all, I
had been trained as a painter. Had I been asked then for
the name of a good illustrator, I should have said
Cruikshank or Doré, while my knowledge of wood-
engraving was limited to Bewick and a few of his
followers. I was not interested in the nineteenth century:
I had only just linked up Hogarth with Swift and Gay,
and was just conscious of the greatness of Blake, and
less conscious of the influence his work had over me at
that time.

I can only remember feeling in a vague sort of way
that I should like to illustrate an important book—it was
a sort of stomach ache—and *The Pilgrim's Progress*
seemed the only book that would lend itself to my
desire to work on something monumental.

While I was passing through this process of gestation,
Robert Gibbings was buying the Golden Cockerel Press
and looking round for wood-engravers who could
illustrate books.

Noel Rooke brought him to see me one day while I
was teaching. Gibbings said he liked my engraving of a
negress that I had shown at the Wood Engraving Society,
and 'would I illustrate a book for him?' My desire to
illustrate evaporated at the idea of doing a real job. My
mind rocked to the point of refusal, when Rooke mur-
mured in my ear, 'Don't you see it is a chance to work
for a man who will really understand and help you?'

I said Yes, suggested *Pilgrim's Progress,* and at the same
moment realized the awful effort to put any of my
dreams into concrete form.

Bunyan, it appeared, was not marketable; neither was *Gulliver's Travels*. After some weeks of delay I was asked to illustrate two volumes of Swift's *Essays*.

The blocks were about two inches square and Gibbings apologized for not being able to pay more than four guineas for each. It was many years before I was to be so well paid again, or to receive an apology for the payment. It is usually reckoned an artist is overpaid—since he is enjoying his work, and is not therefore really working.

I settled down to the first volume of Swift. The first block of this book was my fifth engraving—perhaps this accounted for my nervousness at taking the job on at all. I felt the first block was pretty hopeless and sent it to Gibbings, as I could do no more until he had seen it and either approved or tactfully suggested something else. A prompt reply came back, 'This is jolly good. If you keep this up you'll do well.' I quote the letter to explain how I managed to get through the job. I knew that the block was not too good, and that I could do better in time; but without Gibbings's encouragement I should have been too petrified for further effort.

If it is any encouragement to those in a similar state of nerves on their first job I will add that this awful condition passes off after a while, but the wise student will be more prepared than I was and not wait to learn his craft on an actual job. It is true that my familiarity with Hogarth helped me to get the local colour into the incidents; and I worked my way through the book, feeling conscious that every block was an improvement on the last one, both as engraving and as illustration.

No doubt the long months of thinking about illustration had made my mind adaptable, but even so it was fortunate that my first book was Swift's *Essays* and not *Pilgrim's Progress,* and that the blocks were two inches square and not full-page engravings.

I had collected some books of Gay's *Fables* with Bewick's engravings, and these influenced my technical approach. I discovered the beauty of simple tints from his blocks and bought a tint tool. It was some time before I realized that few of his tints are made up of straight lines, but consist of what is known as the 'wriggle' tint.

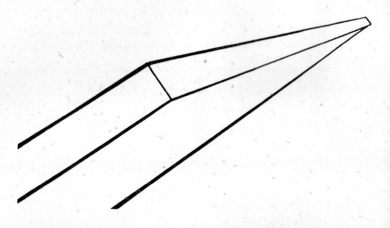

The tint tool is shaped to make a line of even thickness from the moment it enters the wood to the completion of the line. The heel of the tool is graded to the required thickness of the line. It does not bury itself into the wood as the other tools do—in fact, the secret of good tint work is to keep the tool as near to the surface of the block as possible. A different tool is used for the different thickness line; a wide range is available, from the finest possible line to that which is almost the width of a narrow square scorper.

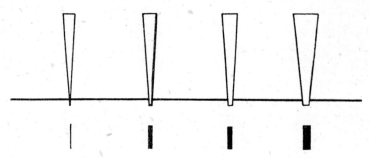

It will be seen—more easily from the wide tool—that the point is square, which explains why it does not pass through the wood so easily as the graver. The section is steep, which means that the engraved line is clean, and need not go so deep to print well.

This is as well, for it is not easy to force any tool deep into the wood and preserve an even line, and even less so the tint tool.

A fine tint is sometimes achieved more easily with a graver by skimming it along the surface of the wood, but it produces a rather shallow line which is not so easily printed as the deeper line of the fine tint tool.

Flat tints, when used to excess, can become dull and mechanical: imagination and a sense of decorative values are necessary to give them life and beauty. Bewick must have realized this danger since he made most of his tints wriggle. The slight tremor in the lines gave a sparkle that can never be achieved with straight lines. He dropped the 'wriggle' for very smooth, polished, or curved surfaces.

In actual fact, the 'wriggle' tint becomes as dull and mechanical as straight lines, and one realizes that the tint tool was used a lot too much. The more one looks at the old engravings the more one longs for inventiveness in the engraving of simple planes.

Bewick was happy when he was engraving animals, for their textures were more varied and the subjects themselves suggested the different textures. The figures he put in were so small as to avoid any important problem of engraving, while his trees and landscapes were reduced to a formula that was the convention of his time, and in these he was content to repeat himself.

Skies were always horizontal lines, broken only by the cloud forms which were shown with curved lines.

He did not engrave at all in a creative sense, as Blake did. Bewick was either imitating the drawing of his time in his landscapes, or imitating the texture of animals. It is a mistake to call him a creative engraver, but we must admit that he created engraving. He paved the way for the modern engraver, and he is an eternal lesson in the importance of getting textures from nature rather than superimposing arbitrary qualities or textures on to the forms.

He is the great craftsman: forcing the tool to express his understanding of his subject, and, in so far, he is creative.

And if he did accept the conventional drawing of his time in his backgrounds, we must remember that few of us escape doing likewise.

Imagination played a very small part in his work, if we compare him with Blake, who was an example of an artist overcoming the difficulties of a craft through sheer drawing and fantasy.

In Bewick nothing disturbs the simple serenity of the
direct statement, and, because his blocks were small and
his technique bold, his engravings achieve a beauty and
vitality that will never fade. He is the starting-off point
for every student of engraving. He varied the direction
of his flat tints only to explain perspective: he attempted
little else. I do not think he was conscious of the decorative value of his tints. He used them because his drawing
did not suggest any other way of expressing flat planes.

Wood-engraving by Thomas Bewick for 'Æsop's Fables'

And so, while he was the father of creative engraving,
he was also the forerunner of imitative engraving.

The twentieth century recognizes him as pointing the
way to creative engraving, but his followers saw his
method as a means for the imitating of tones. His tones

and textures were imitated and perfected by them, and one can trace a steady movement towards perfect tool work through the eighteenth century, resulting in the tone-engraving of the nineteenth century.

Portrait of Shakespeare. Engraving from 'The Penny Magazine', 1832, enlarged from 2 in. wide

Frontispiece from 'Cabinet of Useful Arts for Young Persons', 1832, enlarged from 2½ in. wide. These two blocks show the development of tone engraving and the 'wriggle' tint

Detail of illustration from 'The Pictorial Times', 1846, showing further development of tone engraving, twice enlarged

Detail from same newspaper, showing imitation of pen drawing, twice enlarged

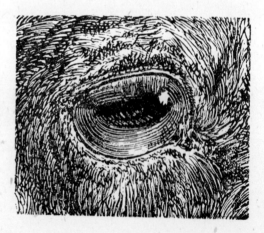

Detail from 'Pictorial Times', 1847, enlarged from 2⅕ in. wide

The habit of using horizontal tints for skies spread into the backgrounds. The engravers, who were translating a wash-drawing made by an artist on the block, used more and more tints, and got further from the idea of drawing direct with the tool. They could not think in terms of drawing, for they were professional engravers. They saw vast areas of sky in straight lines, and even the clouds no longer interrupted the horizontal tint. Variety of tone and form was achieved by varying the thickness of the line, and all the lines wriggle, for wriggle they must if the block was not to become completely mechanical and lifeless.

These engravers developed an incredible sense of tone; they produced engravings that aimed more and more at facsimile reproductions of the artist's painting; and their skill increased. This was inevitable, since the wood-block was the only method of making blocks that would print with type. The artists accepted the craft as a method of reproduction and did not attempt to use it in any other way.

I have in front of me an enlargement of a part of Doré's illustration of Don Quixote guarding his armour. The whole of the background is expressed in horizontal lines, except a few obvious upright forms in the near foreground, which are shown with vertical lines. Horizontal lines show clouds, moon, middle distance and foreground. Tone is obtained with an ingenious varying of the engraved line.

The figure of Don Quixote is distinguished from the background only by the use of a diagonal tint.

And yet, with all this technical monotony, the engraving, enlarged up to four feet, is decorative and has great beauty. One is only just conscious that it is the result of great labour, and that drawing is disappearing, to be replaced by a craft.

To assist the wriggle and give the tones more texture the engravers invented a break or 'stop' in the lines until this in its turn became a monotonous habit, though, for these engravings, a necessary one.

A textbook of 1866 says of these 'stops': 'The dry, hard, wavy and mechanical line seen in old cuts of thirty years ago is now superseded by clouds formed of short lines carefully blended by the pressure of the graver rather than the tint tool. Although different tint tools are generally used, yet the skilful engraver will produce by various degrees of pressure very different lines with one tool—in fact the roundness or fullness of clouds can only be naturally produced by graver-work in short pieces delicately blended together by very fine gravers.'

Detail of 'Don Quixote', drawn by Gustave Doré, engraved by H. Pisan   *Enlarged about twice size*

'One of the most remarkable differences between old-fashioned and modern landscape wood-engraving is the refinement to which the Art is now brought—the old-fashioned engine-turned kind of wave tint being quite superseded by the modern mode of blending short lines, with stops between them. Some of the most exquisite effects are frequently the result of carefully making use of the wood originally left (technically called "stops") in the first working of the sky tints. Of course this presupposes taste and artistic feeling on the part of the engraver, as well as careful manipulative skill. . . .'

In reading the quotation above it does not need much understanding to realize that what might be mistaken at first for pomposity is dignity and sincerity, and these qualities come through the laboured work of the period.

Tone engraving went on evolving ruthlessly, until everything was shown in horizontal or vertical lines, while tones became more and more subtle as the engravers became more skilful at their job of deception. Finally, the eye began to accept an engraving as a wash-drawing.

A few stunts appeared such as those engravings consisting of one long continuous line revolving in a spiral from the centre outwards, and varying in thickness, to show the modelling. These are as interesting as the portraits of Queen Victoria drawn in line which, on close inspection, prove to be words in small type that read as the history of that remarkable Queen's reign. It is a form of exhibitionism that dies of its own inertia.

By the 'nineties engravers were skilful enough to enter into competition with their new rival—the halftone block—and this was the swan song of reproductive engraving. After supplying books with blocks for four centuries the engraver had to give way to the camera.

Detail of drawing by J. G. Pinwell.
Engraving by Swain, 'Once a Week', 1867

Detail from illustration in 'Sunday at Home', 1881, enlarged about three times. It is easy to see the increased skill and tone sense of the engraver—he is almost ready to compete with the halftone block. Competition with the line-block is shown by the engraving on the opposite page from the same magazine

Enlarged from 2⅖ in. wide

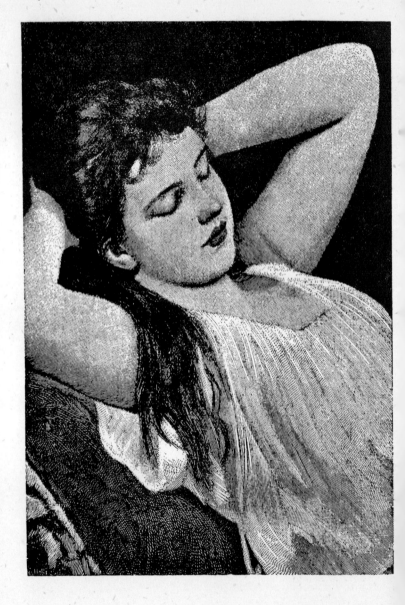

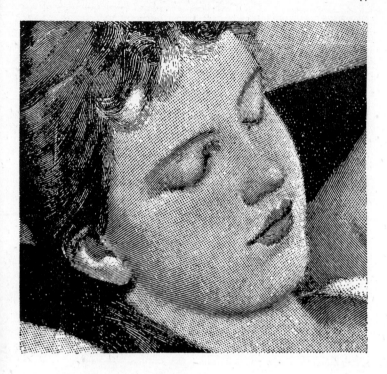

These two illustrations from 'The Girl's Own Paper', 1890, show an active competition with the halftone. The block on the left is enlarged about twice size. In this same magazine is a mixture of line-blocks and halftones used at the same time with the wood engravings that closely resemble both these photo-mechanical methods. It is a sad struggle to see, on the part of the engravers, for their blocks are so much more beautiful than the drab halftones of this date and the line-blocks of careless pen drawings

'Girl's Own Paper', 1898, enlarged from 2½ in. wide

Halftone in same magazine enlarged from 1¼ in. wide

Can we conclude, therefore, that Bewick was also the
father of the halftone block? We must do so, if we
admit that he discovered how subtly graded tones could
be made on a relief block.

And now that we have seen the mechanical tint work of
wood-engraving die a natural death in the halftone, let us
go back to Bewick and see that his tints have great beauty,
and the nineteenth-century blocks for that matter.

*Enlarged
about
twice size*

Detail of wood-engraving by Thomas Bewick for Gay's 'Fables'

'Penny Magazine', *1832, enlarged from 3 in. wide*

'Pictorial Times', *1847, enlarged from 2 in. wide*

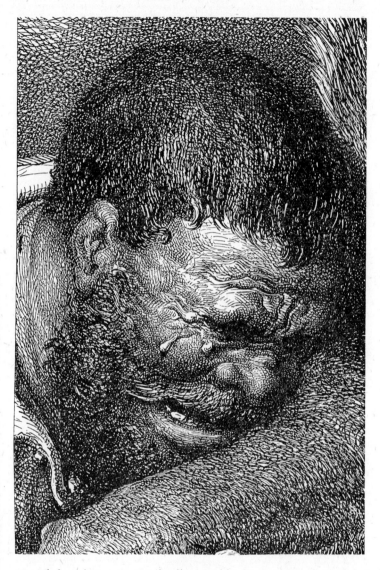

*Detail from 'Don Quixote', illustrated by Gustave Doré, engraved
by H. Pisan, enlarged from 3 in. wide*

'The Gardener's Magazine', 1866, enlarged about twice size

'*The Young Ladies' Journal*', *1882, enlarged about twice size*

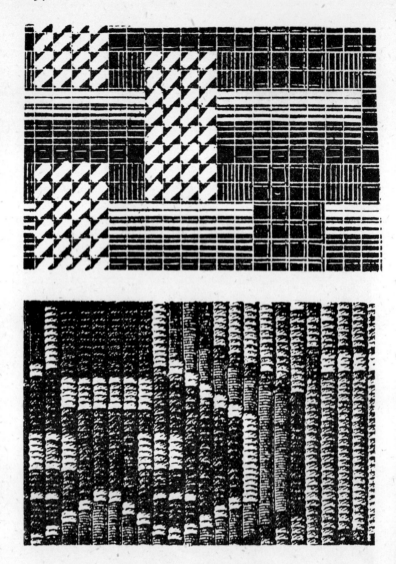

*Needlework designs of 1859 (top) and 1882 (bottom) compared;
both enlarged twice size*

These tints may be appreciated for their beauty alone, and so the tint tool must not be discarded because of its misuse. Apart from its tone the direction of a tint has significance in a design: it can express a mood, it can build up and support the composition. It can strike an arbitrary note, playing on a design as syncopation in music. With the difficult and mechanical device of the wriggle removed it can express austerity and give a sense of space in what might otherwise be a turbulent and over-redundant design. The very regularity of the tint tool is its beauty, for it is a proud line that starts as it intends to finish, and finishes as abruptly as it starts.

The round scorper will make a bold tint, but it tends to make a treacherous start. It has, however, the effect of a graded tint, which is sometimes useful.

I used tints in Swift's *Essays* much as I found Bewick using them, apart from the wriggle; my blocks were small, as his were, and I tackled no problem that he

*Early state of engraving
for 'Swift's Essays',
Golden Cockerel Press*

had not already attempted. Sometimes my preliminary drawing suggested a quality that I attempted to imitate, but I felt when I did so that I was using the medium in the wrong way. I had a strong feeling in those days that engraving was a thing apart from drawing. I have since learnt that to adapt, or translate, a quality of drawing is part of the business of creative engraving.

I had no conscious method when I illustrated my first book: I made the engravings, one by one, and dropped them into position in the type and hoped for the best. It was truly fortunate that I did not start off on *Pilgrim's Progress*—a book that I still hope to do, but with a very different attitude towards the problem of illustration than I had at that date.

By the time I had finished the first volume of Swift I had become an enthusiast over the possibilities of wood-engraving. I was keen to start the second volume, and went for a summer holiday dreaming of infinite tones and textures, when one day the news came from Gibbings that a thunderstorm had destroyed half of the edition of 400. The books had not been insured and the type was distributed. It was too expensive to reset and print again, and it would not pay to print only 200 of the companion volume, so the second book was off!

Alas for the young man who marries on £80, only to find that an act of God has deprived him of half of his capital, while the other half is already spent on a table and some chairs! Beautiful chairs, it is true, but see where museum habits lead us. Beauty is not always expensive to purchase, but on that occasion it was:

'You were mad, my dear fellow, to spend all that money on a table and chairs!'

'But I love them; they are good to look at, and comfortable to sit in.'

'Perhaps. But you have no cups and saucers, and no dustbin!'

'No, that is true.'

And what is this beauty, that is such a cure for depression: the something that flows out and gives such an added sensation of living?

A small pot will renew our sense of form; a book will invoke a fresh world of ideas; a painting will take a skin from our eyes, giving us a fresh vision. Because of this power of rebirth that beauty has, art is one of the great social forces. If our last sixpence is spent on the junk heap we are rich, if we find something that will raise our spirits.

The most serious deficiency in the modern world lies in its lack of appreciation of beauty: we may make excuses, but it is useless to think that anything else is responsible but ourselves; for the sense of beauty is within mankind, and is not a definable thing that can be imposed upon an article at will.

Beauty is God—everyman's, not any one man's God— whether he admits it or not. Beauty is a profound need; it is a belief in that need, and beauty springs from that belief. Beauty is an instinct. Are we losing that instinct? If so we are losing the ability to express our deepest self and we must become inarticulate and vulgar.

The crafts have preserved the sense of beauty in men; the very tools and materials possess beauty. Tools are the vehicle of beauty, and through them a craft becomes a thing of beauty.

The scientist, and even some quarrelsome people, will

tell me that I have not yet defined beauty. I had no intention of defining it, for, thank God, it is one of the undefinable things. Man will go on making God in his own image; we must all find beauty in our own way.

I can say that a tool possesses beauty; a musician will love his violin, and a painter his brushes. A tool, to an artist, is part of his living, speaking self; it is his voice. He cannot possess it—he can only respond to it. If he ceases to respond, the tool will cease to speak, then it is wise to sleep.

Samuel Butler wrote that when his mind refused to work he used his pen slowly and with a care to the making of beautiful forms. His mind relaxed and slept while he enjoyed the sensation of the craft of writing until, refreshed, his ideas began to flow again. We must all sleep in our own peculiar way. Some people think— some sit—some do a little painting. The walls of our public galleries are covered with the relaxation of minds exhausted with the effort of living and thinking.

'Don't you just love to paint? It's such fun!'

'I always do some sketching on my holidays.'

'It must be nice to illustrate books and not to have to work.'

Let the busman and the postman and the General piddle and paint, but don't let's get art mixed up with hobbies. I have nothing against hobbies, you know— saved many an awful row in the home, etc., but God save King George from the amateur.

The years between my first and second book were filled with experiments and experiences too varied to record, and too personal to be interesting. Had it not been for the Wood Engraving Society and its Annual Show I should have ceased to engrave, for I was more interested in paint. I continued to make prints that can only be called 'collector's prints' for want of a better term. I realize now that these prints offer the best scope for experiment, since the engraver is not tied down by the limitations of book-making.

Every engraver should make prints apart from illustration, for it is in these prints that he makes his technical discoveries and develops his drawing and design. And, perhaps, most important of all, he discovers whether he has anything personal to say. All these things find their way into his book work, to add that quality of imagination and drawing that distinguishes him from the purely graphic illustrator.

It is not advisable for any artist to be always working within strictly limited areas. Limitations have produced great works, no doubt, but the greatest artists have not accepted them without question.

The limitations of a craft must always be strained, at times to breaking point, before any real progress can be made. The wisdom of the past is not necessarily the wisdom of the future. A craft must possess the quality of eternal youth, and be ready at any time to pass into a new state of being.

And so, let no man set out to be an illustrator without he has something to say beyond that which is found in a book. He must be an artist who is a designer and craftsman and ready to apply himself to books.

In France, some of the best artists have been asked to illustrate books, and they are not above doing so;

in England the public and the publisher are not so enlightened, nor are the artists so willing.

As a result of making prints I became interested in the craft and studied its development and origin, of which I knew very little. I became interested in wood-cutting, the forerunner of wood-engraving. I abandoned engraving for a while and bought some gouges, a knife, and a side-grain block. The woodcut illustrations in the early books did not interest me so much as the Japanese print, and I launched into a five-colour block, adapting a painting for the purpose. After this my curiosity led me to find out for myself whether it was possible to leave up, 'in relief', as fine a line as the Japanese had done on the side-grain. If I was not entirely successful, at least I discovered that the knife was as delicate as the graver. Rooke told me I had not wasted my time if I had discovered this. The idea, so prevalent in the arty world, that those 'nice, careless, crude prints must be woodcuts', I decided was absolutely wrong—it was the opinion of the amateur.

I printed in varnish inks, as I decided I was too European to print in the Japanese manner. I have always refused to teach the Japanese method of cutting or printing: partly because it must produce derivative work, and partly because I have never used it myself. The Japanese print is the product of three experts: the artist, the cutter, and the printer. The drawing was made on thin tissue and pasted on the block, thus being destroyed when cut by the block-maker, who simply cleared away all the space between the lines. A glance will show that these prints are facsimiles of brush draw-ings. The printer was as highly specialized, for the method is as meticulous as it is possible for any craft to be, and, incidentally, as difficult.

The perfection of the Japanese prints, that is almost inhuman, was the outcome of the intensive specialization of a team of craftsmen. They reveal the Oriental temperament in their fastidious sense of finish and complexity.

It is always a surprise to me that they are so modern—they were produced in the eighteenth century—and that the best period covered so short a time, about fifty years.

It seems futile for a European to make any attempt to work in the same method, especially in the printing. The Western method of printing with varnish inks and rollers is obviously more sound, since it is made familiar to us by tradition. As things are, we find it difficult enough to combine the double job of designing and engraving our own blocks without adding the very difficult and exacting craft of printing.

If I escaped being derivative in my printing I failed to do likewise in my cutting and design. It looked sadly Japanese, and the Wood Engraving Society threw it out for this very reason when I submitted it for their Annual Show.

I made two more cuts in black-and-white, and then abandoned cutting for engraving until 1937, when I cut some Underground posters in wood combined with lino and lithography.

I have done so little cutting that I shall not attempt to deal with it exhaustively. The following general remarks will enable a beginner to go as far as I have done myself; beyond which it might be advisable to discover a book that is devoted entirely to wood-cutting.

M

TOOLS AND MATERIALS

The knife

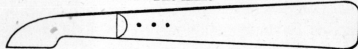

Gouges (round and V)

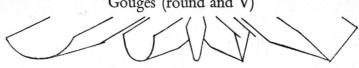

Mallet

V stone

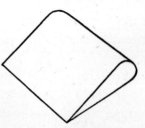

Side-grain wood—pear, maple or cherry.

These tools and materials take the place of those in wood-engraving, otherwise the materials are the same. Generally speaking, cutting lends itself to broader and simpler work than engraving (see the early book blocks and Japanese prints). The stroke with the gouge is more straightforward than that of the knife, since it removes the wood in one cut, but it is not suitable for everything. Even when sharp, the gouge is liable to tear the grain, while the knife is cleaner in its cut and gives greater variety to the drawing.

The principle of using the knife must be familiar to everybody who has carved his name on the school desk: the crudity of these efforts is simply due to poor craftsmanship. Who would object to the carved initials one sees everywhere if the letter-forms were beautiful and the craftsmanship superb? would it still be looked upon as vandalism, I wonder?

The knife forms an oblique angle with the wood and is held rather as a pen is held in writing. The first stroke will show no result as far as printing is concerned, apart from the suggestion of a thin bruised scratch.

The second cut is made with the knife at an opposing angle, so that its point will meet the bottom of the first cut, which is under the surface of the wood. Simply stated, the result is a V-section. If the strokes have been made to meet at each end of the line the wood will lift out of its own accord and leave the following shape.

This shape will vary according to the way the knife is used and the number of cuts that are made.

The last diagram is a detail of my pseudo-Japanese print. It was cut entirely with the knife. Four strokes with the gouge have been added. 1, V-gouge; 2, round gouge (two sizes); 3—narrow round gouge.

From this it will be seen that the knife has certain advantages over the gouge, which can only make the shape corresponding to its section.

The preparation of drawings and blocks is similar to that of wood-engraving.

The gouges must be kept very sharp or the lines will be ragged. It is not easy to sharpen the gouges, as the shape of the cutting edge is easily destroyed. The burr on the inside edge must be removed carefully by the V-stone; the pointed edge for the V-gouges and the rounded back for the U-gouges. Stroke the stone carefully down towards the cutting end of the tool.

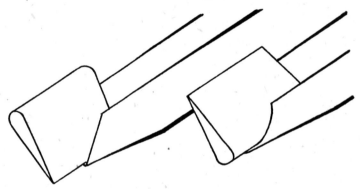

The minimum of cross-hatching should be used, as side-grain wood does not stand up to too much usage.

To clear the larger spaces of wood use a gouge and knock with the mallet. This is quite a delicate process and similar in feeling to wood-carving.

It is well to assume that the block is going to print 'solid'. It is true that some very attractive effects are achieved by bad printing, but these effects can never be repeated, while the object of a block is, after all, that it should be a means of duplicating a certain known effect. When a cut is made for a book-jacket or poster it is possible to take one of these happy effects of bad printing and reproduce it by photography, thus making the print an original. Normally, it is sound to print in as straightforward a way as is possible, and achieve all the effects through the drawing and cutting.

Lino cutting is a very similar process, the same tools being used; but it is easier, as the lino is so much softer than wood. For this reason it is given to children to cut, but this does not mean that it is not capable of fine effects. It is eminently suitable for big simple work; its chief drawback is its softness. It is not possible to leave up fine black lines on a white ground without risking damage in cutting or printing.

COLOUR PRINTS

The drawing is made with an eye to the colour separation; if five printings are to be used it should be seen that the job can be managed in five blocks. Only experience will show how much can be achieved by overprinting these colours to extend the colour range in the print.

There is usually one colour that acts as a key to the others, and this should be drawn and cut first. The drawing is laid on the block in any of the methods described in this section on engraving, and $1\frac{1}{2}$ inches left down two sides.

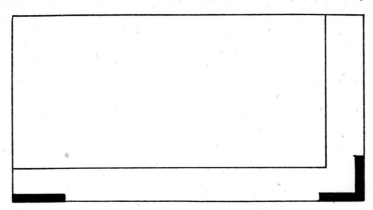

This space is for the key corners that are necessary for registering the other colours. The key corners are placed as shown in the previous diagram and are cut carefully, since on their accuracy depends the ultimate registration.

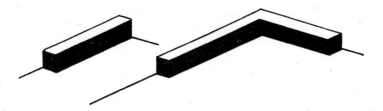

When this block is cut a juicy print is taken and offset on to the next block by putting it through the press.

The second colour or block can then be drawn and cut to fit the first colour and the key corners are cut as before. This process is repeated, offsets of the key being taken each time. It is possible to build up the offset with more than one colour if absolutely necessary. In a simple design it is not necessary to take offsets if the colour shapes are traced carefully enough.

When all the colours are cut, one of the blocks is proofed—the order of printing must be determined by the artist according to the effect he desires. Since some inks are more opaque than others the order of printing will affect the result: for instance, a beautiful green is achieved by printing yellow on top of black, while black will completely obscure the yellow if printed on top.

When the first print is taken the key corners should be trimmed off.

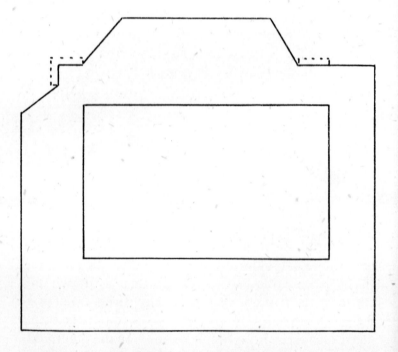

When the next colour is printed, the trimmed corners are placed into the key corners of the block; this should put the print in the correct position for perfect register.

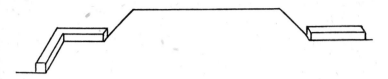

This registration of colours by key corners is only necessary when the artist is making his own prints. For ordinary book work the printer is guided by the original drawing.

I do not think it is pedantic to insist on the difference between wood-engraving and wood-cutting. An etcher would not dream of confusing his process with that of metal-engraving. I have always thought it odd that it should be necessary to explain the difference: the name alone seems to explain so much. But I have heard an otherwise intelligent man say that he would never know the difference, and this after it had been most carefully explained. And quite recently I saw, on the cover of one of our well-known cultural weeklies, a modern 'engraving' that was described as a 'cut', while inside that same number was an old Chinese 'cut' that was called an 'engraving'—the date alone should have told the editor that it could not be an engraving.

Is it possible that men have so lost touch with the sense of craft that its very name implies no more than Greek does to the average man?

While I was making experiments in cutting and engraving prints that had no place except in a collector's folio I had no concern for illustration. When my first book failed to produce a successor the idea of making illustrations ceased to occupy my mind to any great extent. When I was not teaching and painting—I made very few blocks—I was wondering how to pay the rent, this being a more absorbing and often more difficult job than that of applying colour to canvas. It did not occur to me to go in search of work, as I had no knowledge of the publishing world: it did not exist for me, as I never bought, or even looked at, books that were not in the 2d. boxes.

I had no confidence in my ability to illustrate books in general, and therefore saw no reason for calling on publishers. I was unable to make specimens as, in those days, I had little or no knowledge of type. In fact, I continued to drift in a sea of experiment, as I had done since I left the studio at Balham some seven years previously.

But to drift has certain advantages, for one gets into strange waters that would otherwise be unexplored. I wandered through streets and museums and made more unexpected discoveries from having no set purpose than if I had been working to schedule.

I found for myself how each century left its mark on the arts and crafts. I discovered in the airs and graces of the eighteenth century the beauty that I had become familiar with through the writers of that period. There is much to be said for elegance when it is coupled with a robust humour, and I found in the work of this period, in spite of its sinister note, a frank parade of beauty and easy wit that might easily have held one captive.

Perhaps it was as well that I did not go on illustrating Swift and Stern as I had wanted to, or I may have become a confirmed stylist in those early years. I get a recurring nostalgia for the eighteenth century, but I have lost the desire to imitate Hogarth and Rowlandson : they have taken their place on a kind of backcloth in my mind.

Beginning at the early examples of the crafts, I found myself working steadily through the centuries, until now I confess to being immersed in the nineteenth century for everything except domestic architecture, although the early nineteenth-century architecture was almost good. Perhaps one day I shall appreciate what is known as the really modern in the domestic crafts. I find it difficult to surround myself with an architect's idea of design in the home, for that is what it seems to be. Perhaps I am not to get beyond the nineteenth century, but there is also a possibility that one's fears may be confirmed, and that the early twentieth century has not produced much that will be accepted by future generations as good design, except bathrooms and kitchens. However, it seems inevitable that appreciation and understanding of form and design must begin at the early forms, and it seems as inevitable that real interest must move forward and progress just as the forms themselves have progressed to their latest stages.

And so the early forms must be looked upon as a starting off point for the student, not a resting place.

I found, in studying the Greek Vases, that the early ones were the easiest to appreciate. The more familiar I became with them the more I liked the later, sophisticated productions, and this applied to everything in which I became interested.

The outcome of a general interest brings a realization of the inevitable progress of the creative spirit and a distaste for archaic imitation. How much real knowledge

one absorbs it is difficult to say, but I found Shaw
constantly referring to this background of art when
directing the drawings for the *Black Girl,* and I am
certain I was able to understand his point of view more
easily as a result of these wide interests.

Did I choose the path of variety or was it an accident
that my interests and work have been so varied? Was I
preparing myself unconsciously for the variety of books
I was to illustrate by an education that was quite the best
I could have had, or did my interests flow out and find
some place in the mind of publisher or author by a
process of imposition?

It would be interesting to know for certain whether
we have only to think hard enough for a thing to
happen.

It is a commonplace when the thinking and bringing
to life concerns only one person—the artist is the obvious
example; but do other people really react as I think they
do, or is it just a fantasy of my own? I know a man who
writes 'I want £20' many times on a sheet of paper,
and he says it comes along just in time. I have had dreams
of books I have wanted to do, and many of them have
materialized. Say it is chance if you like, I am not really
interested in the argument; I admit to believing something and will leave it at that.

1926–1927 appears to be the year that I started keeping
a careful record of my earning capacity, and I find that
in this year I earned £47 apart from teaching—and this
was five years after I had ceased to be a student. It was
fortunate that I had taken so kindly to teaching.

When I finally decided that I must leave Rugby I

went to F. V. Burridge, then Principal of the Central
School, and explained that I must come back to London.
He asked me if I would come back to teach part-time at
the Central for a fee that was half my Rugby salary.

Remembering that the streets of London were paved
with gold I accepted his offer, feeling sure that I could
make up the deficit quite easily. I did so, but by extra
teaching and not by drawing as I had hoped.

In 1926 I took a job at a small public (?) school near
London which supplemented my income sufficiently
to make me endure teaching art to an even grubbier set
of small boys than I had handled at Rugby; and this I
continued to do, one day a week, for two years.

Why did I do it if I loathed it?

I met a friend a few days ago who said, 'I can't afford
to live in my flat, and I can't afford to move!'

One day a week seems very little to those who spend
every day of the week on a job they loathe, but I
dreaded this Wednesday of teaching from the beginning
of Tuesday morning, and from Wednesday mid-day
suffered from indigestion until Thursday night. Thus
the effects of one day spoilt three days of my week.

I discovered how fortunate I had been at Rugby in
having even a temporary hut with a tin roof in which
to teach art, for in this school the only space in which
I could teach was the dining hall. As large as a church, it
was cold in the winter and lethargic with years of meals
in the summer. Regularly on Wednesdays I ate steak
and kidney pie and rice pudding—except in Lent, and
there I draw a veil over my memory. The staff, collected
round the table overlooking the grim spectacle of a mob
of feeding boys, seemed to change every term. I once

asked a newcomer—a parson—who sat next to me what subject he taught, just to make conversation. The answer came pat: 'Everything but Mathematics'. I felt very depressed, since I could only teach drawing, and was even uncertain of that. Conversation languished. 'Has anyone seen the cricket scores?' Bless the Australians for filling a deadly gap.

The staff envied me for living in the outer world and looked forward to my weekly visit. I was a spot of Bohemia: the whole of London's gay night life, including the underworld and racket of studio life, was embodied in my appearance.

We gathered in their rooms after lunch, and while we drank Camp coffee they asked for news and spicy adventurous stories. I did what I could to cheer them up—I admit to pulling their legs a little and playing up to the character they had given me: it would have been heartless to refuse. On the occasion when I doubled their Derby Sweep and won it they were convinced even more that I was a tough case of art and craft. After all, I could hardly expect them to know that I was too absorbed in the problem of existence to know anything about gay life.

I taught 'art' at the far end of the hall with such tables as could be spared. I was allowed no materials beyond pencil and paper, 'for boys are so wasteful and messy, y'know'.

I circumvented these restrictions by importing materials that did not need water pots or brush. The boys often worked hard, and some even showed considerable talent, but what chance had they in such a dour and grudging setting?

If any such school reads this account and has an uneasy
conscience with regard to its methods of teaching art,
I beg of it to face up to one of the most important
problems of modern civilization. Art is so often looked
upon as the Cinderella of education. At the moment, it
is true, there is a 'drive', and the art education of this
country is being reorganized; but the movement does
not touch these schools, for they do not come under the
authorities concerned with progress; and yet it is in
these schools that so much talent is to be found. Young
boys, fresh and eager to learn, with minds that are
thirsting for good things, are made cynical and
disillusioned before they reach middle school. It is no
wonder that a boy is ashamed of having good taste, when
the whole atmosphere of his school and its staff is one
of indifference and contempt.

While art is treated as a form of slackness and im-
morality by a group of bored and repressed men, we
can expect nothing but cynicism and a distrust of
anything to do with beauty. Teaching art in schools is
not so much teaching boys to be artists as making them
future citizens with some concern for their welfare.

Niggard housekeeping, repression, vulgarity, pedan-
try, questionable kippers and blobs of porridge, stained
glass windows of doubtful heraldry, forms and tables
that would be discarded by an up-to-date cow-house—
this was the atmosphere in the hall where I was asked to
teach art—and the air was never changed.

The boys were unable to relax in their one short
period of *art* per week for fear the head might walk in,
though I did my best to break through the grim
tradition. I succeeded best on the occasion when, having

set them to work quietly one afternoon, I developed a very demonstrative attack of hiccoughs that echoed through the hall. For a long while they restrained themselves, when at last a head was raised and the boy's eye caught mine and we grinned at one another. I explained it was the steak and kidney pie, and the whole class relaxed into hysteria. The head walked in—my attack passed off in the effort I had to make to justify such a scene. I explained that I was lecturing on humour in art —his face relaxed a little, for he read *Punch*. I was never able to find out whether he had no sense of humour whatsoever, or whether it was merely out of my reach. I once mentioned to him at lunch that I had noticed a photograph in the paper of his school (X) next to Rugby in the shooting at Bisley. He answered: 'You mean Rugby next to X.' Now was that retort serious or just superb humour?

The fact remains that my account book shows that this school added £90 per annum to my income. It is now only a memory that fills me with indignation of such methods of swindling serious parents who are hoping for the best for their sons. Often enough these parents were old students themselves who had brought their sons back to the 'dear old place' where they spent the happiest years of their lives. Poor men—I longed to warn them, but disappointed men cannot see their youth with any degree of clear vision, and besides, I should have got the sack. . . .

In the summer of 1927 I reached, I suppose, my lowest financial ebb. Contrary to the emphatic declaration of a number of charming people, I did not find the addition of a child to the household a financial asset. Where did that legend come from that a child costs nothing the first two years, in fact one almost saves?

In the middle of the vacation—that grim nightmare of every part-time teacher who does not get paid for the three-months' holiday that the layman envies him so much—I was asked by Macdonald Gill to help in the painting of a church decoration in Sunderland. I blessed the two years I had spent on the mural, even if I felt I had only learned to separate the white of an egg from the yellow, and in three days' time I found myself in the train with no idea of what I would be expected to do. There is little to fear, however, for those who work with Macdonald Gill, for he is most able in making everybody happy and getting his men to work.

In the evening our party went to inspect the church and the scaffolding. We all climbed up, except one man who failed to conquer his fear—he returned after a few days' unsuccessful effort. When I reached the top I lay down on the planks and wondered if I should ever get down again. In a few days we were sliding down the poles instead of using the ladders, and the 'Seven Days of the Creation' appeared on the walls in a few weeks.

When I had finished I felt I should like to do a church single-handed, but another church, like another book, did not seem available. I had the pleasure, however, of making a lasting friend of Gill, and I returned to London with enough money to carry me through.

For the technique of tempera painting I must refer the reader elsewhere. I used Laurie's *Materials of the Painter's Craft* myself and it has been my bible ever since for the study of the craft of painting.

N

I will not enlarge on our adventures so near to heaven in Sunderland: our weekly visit to the melodrama; high teas on Sunday in caves along the coast, where there are 'such quantities of sand' (the original walrus is in the local museum), or watching a wedding from the top of the scaffolding, where I lay on my belly and looked down through the planks to the great annoyance of the lady verger. I was left up there unawares until it was too late to come down, so I sang with the organ, tried to prevent a sweet from falling out of my mouth down on to the altar beneath, and estimated the ground plan of the bride. Had the organ suddenly stopped and left me singing the bridegroom might well have thought it a warning from heaven.

This job formed the bulk of the £47 I earned that year in legitimate labour.

List of other commissions from this year:

Drawing of a Dürer woodcut for the British Museum.

Engraving for a press advertisement.

Roughs (not accepted) for booklet for metal windows.

Label for bales of cotton.

Sale of one print—Two guineas.

It was during this year that I made the resolution to refuse no job of any kind, on the principle that a designer should be capable of undertaking anything and making a sound job of it. I have kept to this resolution, even if I have not always been successful in its principle, and so it was not on my own initiative that I ultimately drifted into books.

1927–1928 showed an increase of £39 2s. 3d. on the previous year.

Most of this year's total was accounted for by my second book, which I illustrated just three years after my first one.

In the spring of 1927, Rooke once more steered a publisher my way. Basil Blackwell wanted an engraver to make some decorations for Pindar's *Odes* in two volumes, to be printed by the Shakespeare Head Press. Once more the background of the book was familiar to me and easily accessible, for I had long been acquainted with the Greek Vases in the British Museum, and in particular those contemporary with Pindar that were actually the prizes for the games that the *Odes* were written around.

Bernard Newdigate sent me some pages of type with spaces left for the headings to each ode. These were double spreads, the translation facing the original Greek, and so my problem was simple enough. The vases supplied the decorative approach. The period, 400 B.C., was too well known for any liberties to be taken, and yet not well enough known to allow me to get away from the vases to any appreciable extent—at least in my then present state of enlightenment.

And so I spent days drawing from the vases, discovering the subjects and legends of the odes. This is known by the vulgar as 'cribbing'. I call it respect for tradition, though I must admit now that perhaps I showed too much respect for tradition about this time and not enough initiative of my own. I find the two volumes show quite clearly how my interest moved from the early period to the later, which, I believe, is called 'the decadence' by discerning people. The extra freedom and sophistication, and often exquisite drawing I found in them, gave me more pleasure than the early rather formal figures.

But I have never yet done a book of any length that has not shown a change of approach towards the end. It is only when one is finishing a book that one learns how it should be done, and the next book is a new problem. Therein lies the fascination of books. Books are individuals. The illustrator has not learnt his job on one book —or sixty for that matter. He must start again on every book—perhaps a little more able every time—possibly with more sympathy—but it is always a fresh start. This individual life of each book means that the illustrator must grow into his subject and, as time is limited, he must grow into it in the course of the job. The transition is usually less obvious to other people than to the artist himself, and it serves to keep the book alive.

No illustrator should look upon himself as a machine that has to turn out a certain number of drawings in exactly the same style, just because they are all in one book.

My designs in Pindar were influenced by the vases of every period. They were based on line drawings and engraved as if they were cuts—in fact the whole job was a mix-up in an effort to achieve a certain end. In spite of this the translator—a very charming man whom I visited in the South Downs—was pleased, and the publisher and the printer still say they are proud of the books I was doing for them at that period.

Perhaps it was a process of rationalization that made me enthusiastic over black line engraving. It was fortunate for me that I was so, for it was no joke clearing away so much wood. I suspect also that I was influenced by the very beautiful blocks that Eric Gill was engraving for the Golden Cockerel Press at that time.

Bernard Newdigate was only too pleased to find an engraver who was prepared to waste so much wood, and for the next three years I worked almost exclusively for the Shakespeare Head Press, and my week-ends in Oxford are still a pleasant memory of long, easy discussions on printing, illustrating and producing fine books. My long-pent-up desire to have a hand in the making of books was released by this atmosphere of learning and good humour, and I discovered myself talking with conviction on how books should be illustrated as if I were an expert.

The blocks for Pindar were produced under exacting conditions, for Blackwell was in a hurry to publish and I had to reduce the time element to the minimum. Perhaps that is why I attempted no more than the vases suggested. It happened, fortunately, that the simple lines harmonized perfectly with the bold Greek type. My feeling for book work was more instinctive than practical, although it is true that I was already beginning to have those long talks with J. H. Mason, and had possibly absorbed more than I thought for at the time. It comes back to me that I was rather insistent that the engraving should balance the weight of the type perfectly and that I was prepared to do battle with any engraver who used the 'white line method'. One phrase I was very fond of using was 'the architectural quality of a built-up line'. This was, of course, in my case an incorrect phrase; I had borrowed the idea from the craft of lettering with its building up of a pen or brush letter form, and had adapted it to the action of cutting away from a line—not building up to it.

Nevertheless, the process of drawing a free line on a block and cutting away with a tool does produce a built-up quality if the engraver is not too obsessed with imitating his drawn line. This is, after all, the beauty of the early cuts, and it was these cuts, as well as Gill's blocks, that gave me my enthusiasm for the black line method. I am still prepared to defend it, even if I have abandoned the method myself. It was fortunate that the short period in which I was prepared to work in this style coincided with Pindar.

Blackwell's amusing and encouraging comments helped me through a very hot summer; for I had to produce one block a day. From a sketchbook full of studies I produced the design in the morning, engraved it in the afternoon, and 'cleared' it after tea sufficiently for Lawrence to rout the larger spaces with his machine. This was a fairly regular routine, and I learnt as much about clearing wood as I want to.

I was once visiting a commercial engravers' shop and, as I watched a man at work, a proud friend said to me, 'When Bill gets busy you can't see 'im for chips!' I felt much like that myself during this summer.

My studio was the corner of a bed-living room, and my bench a card table that had to be wedged to remain steady. All textbooks say that a rigid table is essential to good engraving! Perhaps they are right, but it was years before I abandoned the card table—Shaw's *Black*

Girl was engraved on it and under the same conditions, which were alleviated, however, by an excellent view of gardens and fruit trees which are now destroyed and covered by a block of flats.

A friend made the charming gesture of presenting me with a good rigid desk later. I exchanged the view for the desk—progress is necessary, apparently—even if it isn't necessary it happens somehow. I am tempted to think that a good view is as necessary as a good studio or a rigid desk.

I admit that a firm table *is* useful, especially when clearing out a lot of wood. It is an arduous job, but the muscles of the wrist and arm become sufficient in time. I have since handed on all clearing to that skilful crafts-man John Beedham, now that I have enough work to justify the small extra expense.

John Beedham is the only man I know who can be trusted to clear a block. An exquisite engraver of the reproduction school, he has recently reissued an excel-lent little textbook on engraving (Faber & Faber) that every engraver should read.

The illustrations of the various stages of the blocks show how important a part the clearing of the back-ground can play.

Towards the end of the second volume I began to lose my interest in the 'built-up quality of the line'. The speed of production invoked a skill that threatened to reduce the lines to a suavity that I felt to be dangerously near dullness. It is not possible, or desirable, to avoid skill in engraving: the only way to preserve the quality that the early cuts had is to cut on the plank as they were

cut, and not engrave them—unless the quality to be desired is suavity.

I was in a quandary, for the Greek line I was after was suave and should have been drawn with a pen or brush. It became clear to me that my approach was wrong somewhere, and my enthusiasm for black line engraving waned—fortunately towards the end of the job. I can now imagine the *Odes* decorated very differently—I wonder if it would be as popular.

The most important thing I discovered in illustrating Pindar was that illustrations to poems should be decorative in treatment and implication rather than graphic. I still believe this to be so, except on the rare occasions when I see a graphic yet poignant illustration that completely upsets all my theories.

Perhaps I am again rationalizing when I say that an illustrator is a servant to literature and should not work in a set style unless he confines his activities to one type of book.

*Paste-up of 'Pindar' blocks showing arrangement as
double opening*

List of other commissions for this year:

Engraved bookplate.

Trade Mark for the Golden Cockerel Press.

Sale of prints—£9 9s. od.

Postage stamps for Postal Congress Union 1929.

The actual payment for this last item occurred in 1929,
and accounts for a very substantial increase in my income for that year—an increase that the Income Tax
authorities could not believe was temporary. A small
group of artists were invited, with four commercial
firms, to submit designs for the stamps, and Burridge,
who had always helped and encouraged me, had put
my name forward. When I heard the names of the other
artists I was convinced I had no hope of success, but I
was to receive an honorarium that seemed to me to be
ample recompense for the work I was to do. I went to

the British Museum and looked at British stamps—
selected those that I admired most and decided to work
along similar lines. I preferred the simple designs that
affected no trimmings. The Post Office had insisted on
an oval of a certain size being left for the King's head, and
this left very little space for unnecessary ornament after
the lettering had been placed to its best advantage. I
decided that my stamps should stand or fall by the
design of the lettering on a plain white ground.

Two of the five values chosen were my designs: it was
a great day when I received the news and a very substantial cheque. The stamp collectors—a race as difficult
to please as farmers—referred to the lack of England's
beauty spots in the new designs, while one more
imaginative critic discovered a resemblance to a beer
bottle label in one of mine.

I liked them myself and still like them, and still think
that lettering on a plain ground can be as decorative and
dignified as any Marble Arch in the corner.

I paid all my debts!

In the Spring of 1929 I exploited my interest in the
black line method to the full when I engraved some
blocks for the Shakespeare Head edition of *Bede*. The
original cuts were so badly printed that it was impossible
to make line blocks from them, and Newdigate asked
me if I would recut them. I refused to cut them, as an
almost buried conscience told me that it was a little too
near mere reproduction, but I agreed to engrave them
if I were allowed a little more licence in translation.
Lawrence photographed the design on to boxwood for
me and I proceeded to translate them. In actual fact
there was little translation of technique. I was so soaked

in the early cuts that I produced blocks that were almost facsimile. I learned an enormous amount in doing this job, but it is a thing that no artist-engraver should do more than once.

Early stage of engraving of cut for 'Bede'

In the summer I illustrated the second volume of Pindar—just one year after the first. It was during this job, while at Oxford for a week-end, that the idea of illustrating Homer was first discussed. I well remember the scene at Mott's house. Blackwell, Newdigate, Mott, Parker—now dead—and myself in the library after dinner—discussions of books—of producing great books, expanding one scheme after another. Oxford is such a good atmosphere for that sort of talk.

Blackwell decided to publish a complete Homer to follow Pindar.

When we started on it in the autumn I discovered that Blackwell had visualized Homer rather as we had produced Pindar. I did not see it that way myself. Homer was an epic: it had intensity, light and shade. I decided that Homer must not look British-Museum-Greek-Vase-room-400 B.C. I went to Oxford to talk it over. My idea was to make a full page block to every book of the *Iliad* and *Odyssey*. I would imply the panorama of the poems by having the various incidents of the book brought together in each block, thus forming forty-eight frontispieces. These were to strike a rich, regular note throughout the four big volumes.

As I talked to Blackwell I saw, in my mind, the dark turmoil of the *Iliad* and the strangeness of the *Odyssey* unfolding in a series of large blocks of troubled and fugitive tones.

It was a glimpse into the future, for it was to be years before I succeeded in getting anywhere near this quality of tone and texture in a job that was to be on an equally grand scale. In fact, this job I have only just completed in September 1938, and is Shaw's *Back to Methuselah*. It will be discussed in its proper place, but I can say here that what I have achieved in *Methuselah* is what I had hoped to do with Homer in the year 1929. For an hour at Oxford I had looked nine years into the future.

Blackwell responded to my excitement, though it meant my fee was doubled; which goes to prove what a publisher will do for the love of books; and if ever a man loved books and the making of them it was Blackwell.

I returned from Oxford triumphant, and yet as the train drew near London my courage slipped away. During the journey I had been trying to evolve a more definite conception than that vision of mine in Oxford, and I was realizing that it was not going to be easy; I was beginning to wonder if I were capable of getting any nearer than that brief glimpse. Although I do not remember lacking imagination in my early days of illustration, I know that I found it most difficult to get anything on to paper. My mind soared, only to be brought to earth with a bump at the first contact of pencil to paper. Yet I cannot blame myself for my enthusiasm at Oxford and my ultimate failure to achieve that which I had thought, for one brief hour, I could do. That glimpse was something that was to be fulfilled in part and, perhaps, will be in full one day.

It was with foolhardy courage that I had plunged into Homer. I had had so little experience to support my ideas, and so little technical achievement behind me. But, after all, a complete Homer was no mean undertaking; it is hardly surprising that I found the first effects a little numbing.

I spent some five or six weeks in intensive reading and

research in order to discover the material that was available for Homer; the poems themselves, like the Bible, proved to contain conflicting accounts of events, clothes and armour. I concluded the search with the consciousness—since so little was known of the period, and of Homer himself for that matter—that I was free to do what I liked. I discovered that the poems were handed down, and added to, by each generation, in order to give them topical tone, which accounted for the many conflicting descriptions that occur in the *Iliad,* sometimes in one line thus: 'The spear pierced his breastplate, but he stepped aside and escaped swift death'. The early method of fighting was to crouch behind a huge shield 'like a tower' and, if a soldier saw a spear coming to pierce his shield, he twisted and so dodged the point. The introduction in the line of the breastplate simply marks the introduction of that item into the soldier's fighting equipment and so replaced the shield. It did not matter if it was impossible to step aside once the spear had pierced the breastplate. The main glory and spirit of the poems remained the same and the audience apparently was not so fussy over details as is our modern generation.

And so I was left to flounder for details and see even the image of Homer dispersed into a host of wandering storytellers marching through the centuries from 2000 to 500 B.C. 1,500 years to choose from, but, unfortunately, no records of anything much before 500 B.C.

It is a mature artist indeed who can cope with such a large work with so few restrictions. Is it odd, then, that when I started the first design I found it a little difficult? For two years I had thought in terms of black line decorations based on 400 B.C. vases; I find that my first blocks to Homer are but little more than elaborated Pindars.

Paste-up of early blocks for Homer

Paste-up of later blocks for Homer, showing increase of tone and texture

And more elaborate, too, was the labour of clearing wood; my evenings for many months were well occupied. It was not entirely my fault that I had not the courage to change my style as completely as I had thought to do—any artist will know how difficult this is and how slowly such a step is taken.

And I do not wish to give the impression that I was dissatisfied with the work at the time or exhausted with the labour, although I realized even then that I was in for two years' work. It is only in retrospect that I can see the colossal labour of cutting away so much wood and feel the exhaustion that must have overcome me at times. When I look at it now I see how far I developed from the designs of Pindar, while at the time I felt them to be disappointingly close.

Innovations often appear so small that they pass unnoticed until retrospection shows them to be revolutions of no mean order.

In the first twelve blocks of the *Iliad* I find many reminders of strange experiments in design. The metacube theory was then in the air; I remember an inane thought coming into my mind when it was first explained to me: 'what would a sphere do if it met a cube?'.

This metacube theory, which I cannot now attempt to explain, was absorbed into Homer, and the disease grew until I produced a marvellous design—from the metacube point of view—which proved to be the worst design I had ever made. I abandoned the thrills of geometry and decided to rely on plain drawing and instinctive design. It was obvious I was not ready for such foolproof methods of making designs; neither was I encouraged by the results of the other artists who had

o

been drawn into the movement, in spite of their assurance that all the old masters had used this or similar methods.

In the autumn of this year, 1929, I engraved my first large block, which was, perhaps significantly, in the white line method. I called the block 'Hemlock' (Giant Cow Parsnip), which proves how little I knew of botany. The plant grew in my garden, and for two years I had felt that it should be possible to make something out of it, and had drawn and painted it ready for the moment when I should know what to do. And then one day I saw the sun streaming through the leaves, transforming the plant into a piece of sculpture in black and white. The leaves had the rhythm of Greek draperies, and the urgent stem, that forced its way to the top of the plant to burst into globes like constellations, suggested a quality that could only be found in wood by a graver. I find it necessary to stress the point that I did not make the engraving as a careful botanical study. It is true that I had studies to hand, and that I had watched the plant for some years; but when I did decide to make the engraving it was with the same sudden urgency as the plant itself broke through the ground each spring. No previous engraving of mine showed any indication of the qualities of this block. In size, conception, and tool work, it was a sudden occurrence—at least its appearance was sudden.

I have come to understand technique as something that comes to life when there is a sufficiently urgent demand for it. The birth of technique is so simultaneous with the conception of an idea that we do not easily notice the duality and fusion; there is no need to, but it is important to realize that technique is not a thing separate from feeling, to be imposed on an idea like the coating on a pill.

Technique and conception are one—a form forces its way through the wood; the tool quivers and strains as it becomes part of that same urgency. It has been said that to draw a foot we must become that foot; or a tree, then we must become that tree. It is only another, perhaps more expressive, way of saying that good drawing must have intensity.

It was not as a student of plant form that I made the print called 'Hemlock'. I was more conscious of sculptured draperies and Greek Vases and the struggle of the blacks to dominate the whites; and, above all this wild turbulance of growth, a tremendous tranquillity of design. I was making an independent print, unrestricted by any limitations such as the book was imposing on me at the time: I was not concerned as to whether I would please somebody, or sell even one copy.

The value of such an experiment, apart from the pleasure I derived from making it, convinced me of the necessity of making similar essays into the unknown and unwanted. And since then I have made one of these large blocks almost every year; never more than one a year. Sometimes one of these large blocks is in my mind for two years before I make it. I am afraid they get less and less popular, but then they are not made as 'popular' prints. In them I have made all my discoveries and felt my way to a freedom and invention that needs but little adaptation to be absorbed into my book work.

There is a great need in all of us to break free of convention and restrictions at times, lest we become ridden with routine. I would advise every engraver to make these large blocks—large because most book work is small—and to attack them as if it does not matter whether they are finished, or what they mean when they are finished. A little madness or incoherence is a thing I encourage in all students: it is not good to be always working as a reasonable and intelligent being. Invention is too often the result of a blind instinctive groping—it is often an accident—if anything can be called an accident—that is only appreciated after it has happened.

'Hemlock' proved to be my best seller, although the Academy turned it down while the museums of England and America were buying it.

While I was engraving it I was quite unconscious of all the precepts laid down for good printing. I cut away large whites and left delicate black points unprotected; large black masses were broken with a stipple that almost defied printing. It was the first time I had used stipple since the illustrations to Swift, and the first time that I had used a multiple tool.

When I had finished I realized that I should ultimately abandon the black line method for the white line, and that I should return to the quality of engraving that I had tried out in Swift and visualized for Homer. From then on my designs for Homer became suffused with rich tones, and the printer began to groan with the task of printing them on the heavy hand-made paper.

My record for 1930 shows that Homer occupied my time for the whole year, except for one large cut in two tones of black. This was adapted from an oil painting. The range of tones in an oil makes it a valuable study for

the fullness of values that is possible in a block. I have not followed up this experiment of printing in two tones. There is much to be done in this direction; some old prints, made in two colours that are virtually two tones, are suggestive enough.

The title-page for the set of five volumes of Homer was made in this year. It is, incidentally, a sound plan to design the title-page towards the end of a job, for it should have something of the quality of prophecy about it, and this is only possible when the designer is getting towards the end of a book and knows his material very well.

I went to Oxford to discuss it. Newdigate wanted the portrait of Chapman, and Blackwell was keen on the Shield of Achilles coming somewhere in the book. I had ideas for a double-spread: so many large blocks in a book seemed to call for weight at the beginning. All three ideas were brought together and resulted in a double opening of shield and portrait.

By a happy chance the curved corners on the portrait could be used on the opposite page for the Shield of Achilles—it can be seen how the shield evolved from the frame of the portrait both in shape and texture.

In this engraving I started rocking a multiple tool for the first time; though I did not exploit its possibilities for some years.

Now when I discover a new texture, I follow it up as far as I can, until it leads yet further. Perhaps it is a sign of increasing years that one conserves one's ideas and discoveries to make the most of them. I prefer to think that I was less alive to the possibilities of my medium in the days when I was working on Homer.

A multiple tool is, strictly speaking, an anachronism. It was made for the days when engravers were busy reproducing or copying tones. These tones consisted

Practice block, showing first and subsequent experiments at rocking the multiple. A little practice will show which tool was used and how it was rocked

of a number of parallel lines, so that a tool which could cut two, four or six lines at one stroke had the obvious value of economy.

For such purposes this tool is patently anathema to the modern artist-engraver, who does not demand mechanical perfection and who seldom has the need for a large area of flat tone.

A tool when designed for a particular function has only that function in the eyes of its designer. It takes a later generation to realize its potentialities, when its original purpose no longer exists. A tool will be idle until somebody begins to play with it in a childish fashion; childish because such playfulness is so often

accompanied by the feeling of naughtiness and irrever-
ence towards the teaching and experience of the older
generation.

This playful approach to technique is the essence of
inventiveness : it will always create new life and interest.
Just so will a child make attractive drawings on a black-
board with chalks that were made for writing up the
problems of long division. Blackboards and chalks are
now toys of the nursery, where they will be long after
the school room has abandoned them for some more
efficient method of improving the young mind.

There was a time when I scorned the use of the multiple and ground down the heel of a beautiful nineteenth-
century tool that I possessed to provide me with a wide
square scorper that I could not afford. I now know this
to be a greater act of vandalism than the way I have since
used the companion to this tool, which is now in the
company of several varieties of its kind.

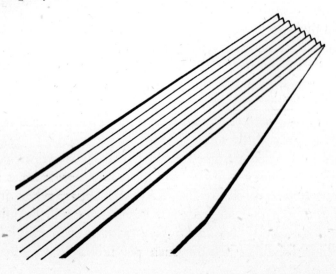

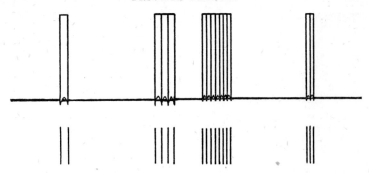

When I used it for the first time in 'Hemlock' it was to obtain a light broken tone in the background. This was achieved by using the tool in a consciously careless way—an easy enough thing to do, since I could not have used it correctly if I had wanted to. It is not easy to keep the tool flat and cutting evenly—the idea of rocking it came to me when I was trying to keep it flat. I found a tendency for one corner to bury deeper than the other.

 With very little thinking I found myself turning this into a regular pattern by rocking the tool as I pushed it and alternating the strokes.

The original copper engraving of Chapman's portrait had a marbled texture in its corners, and it seemed appropriate to use my newly discovered texture, even if it were quite a different one from the original.

It is quite impossible to describe a subtle action concisely, for a careful description will only make the simple seem complicated, and that is an impression I do not wish to give; the action of rocking a multiple is very simple, but in its very simplicity lies the subtlety that cannot be described, and, like all simple actions, it is capable of infinite variation.

The illustrations show the different textures achieved by using the tool in varying positions.

Sometimes the rocking is slow and sometimes rapid; sometimes the tool is held high and sometimes it is held almost flat.

No further description is necessary for an engraver to try it out for himself.

The above illustration shows textures obtained by multiples used in different ways, while the next shows stipples obtained by the picking movement similar to that described in the early part of the book.

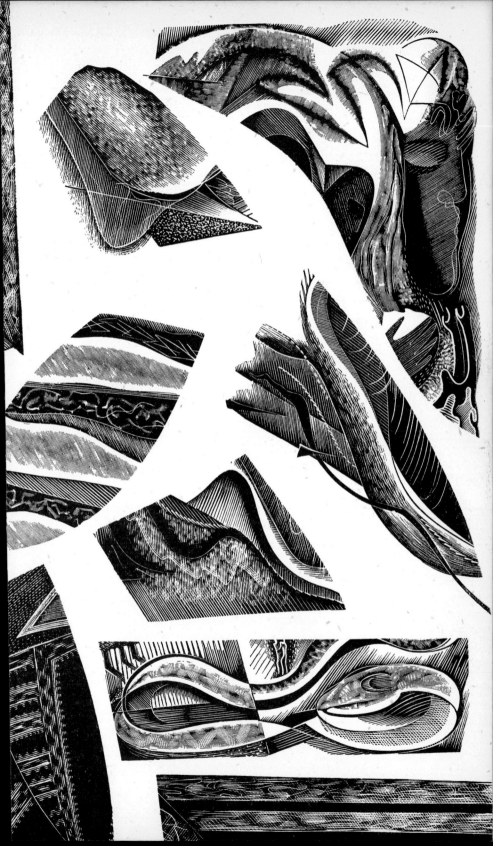

25th September 1938

During the next six days war may be declared! Six days is the time limit set by one man to what may prove to be the peace of the world. And on reading these last pages over I find myself wondering why it is so absorbing, or so necessary, that I should make such careful observations on the minute differences of the textures and stipples that are achieved by using a tool in slightly different ways.

For so many weeks the atmosphere has been charged with war; now the crisis comes nearer every hour. The papers are thundering out their daily warnings to keep calm and quiet: perhaps that is why I go on writing into the early hours of the morning.

Whitehall is crowded again as in the days of 1914: I look at some nineteenth-century engravings and marvel at the peace in them; at the infinite labour that shows such confidence in what is right and proper; an infinite labour that was so worth while. Their deep, patient beauty only emphasises the present universal fear.

When I started this book I doubted whether it would ever be published: now I am wondering whether it will ever be finished. When I re-read part of it to-night there seemed little reason for so much concern over the markings of a tool on a piece of wood. Yet we must keep calm, and surely that calm is to be found in the correct handling of a tool—dignity, too, for that matter.

The enlargement of Doré's engraving looks out from my wall and tells me that such madness as war is cannot happen again: the raucous street cries make me fear the worst. But I must read what I have written on the multiple tool, and pick up the threads again—if only for a while. What matters if the book is never finished, if one can find peace and quiet in writing of a craft that has become so close a friend that one's heart must be torn out to be separated from it to join in a useless slaughter. And what better threads can one pick up than those silvery thread-like lines of the multiple tool!—but I discovered on reading through that I have written all that I wish to about the multiple tool for the time being.

So I must, perforce, return to the making of Homer, that beguiled me into so much chatter about textures.

And, once again, I find that there is little more to say about Homer except that the months rolled on slowly to the September of 1931, when the last block was made, just two years after the first one.

And in this September of 1931, in a peaceful place in Cornwall, came the disturbing news of an economic collapse. Sitting by the sea one reads that small incomes are to be heavily taxed and teaching salaries reduced. The future begins to shrivel, for what is to happen to the brave ventures that Blackwell had planned to follow Homer? For three years I had worked for Blackwell and buried myself in the glowing dust of Pindar and Homer, only to be awakened to the realities attendant on a world economic crisis.

It is hardly necessary to point out that I was totally unsuited to adapt myself to commercial book production. I was completely unaware of its problems.

Homer was finished! I returned to London with a blank programme ahead.

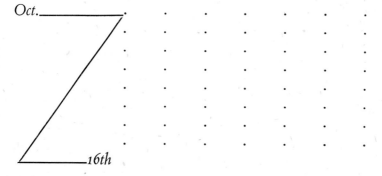

26th September ⎫ London is digging by day and night in
27th September ⎪ parks and squares. Sand is filling the
28th September ⎬ spaces between basement windows and
⎪ walls. Sandbags are piling up against
29th September ⎪ buildings. A large ostrich with as much
30th September ⎭ sand as it needs: or is it enough?

16th October

I must make some comment on this last gap. It is so
definitely a gap in my own mind that it must be recorded
in view of the last entry. There would seem to be little
that can be said of a gap; how describe it? and why
describe it for that matter? But this gap was not only a
personal one: it was universal. It has yet to be seen
whether we can return to normal or how long it
will take.

We are told that there is no vacuum in nature: no gap
that is empty or without form. A blank space is only
according to our way of thinking, seeing, or feeling.
Our senses have missed a few weeks of conscious
activity; we have groped blindly, but instinctively, to
the solid ground of objectivity again, and if that solid

ground seems strange is it to be wondered at? The
ground *is* strange. So strange that we must still be
wondering if the whole fabric of things is but illusion.
The tactile values are gone; we are no longer in touch
and we realize that it is ourselves, that strange mystery
of our innermost self, that has melted into space and
is waiting to find again a semblance of confident
direction.

What has happened these few days? I do not know.
A nightmare is not always remembered except for the
litter of details that fills our mind afterwards with fear
and unhappiness; we must continue to grope in shadows
and hope that exhaustion will bring oblivion, and
oblivion merge into reality again.

I have the early pages of this book to remind me of
what I was doing and where I must pick up my narrative
again. This book must bridge my gap. The last phrase,
written on 25th September, must be the phrase of 16th
October that will carry on with a job that has been
started.

Homer was finished! I returned to London with a
blank programme ahead.

That blank meant more than I cared to admit at the
time. For four years I had worked with Blackwell and
Newdigate in an atmosphere of scholarship, good
humour, and beautiful books. I have said that I had
become unsuited to commercial production: I must
hasten to explain, in case I appear to have blamed Oxford, that my complete absorption in the production of
fine books, Pindar and Homer in particular, had made
it difficult for me to think in terms of the cheaper and

contemporary novel. The transition was too abrupt. I had given no thought to the problems or technique of illustration beyond what was necessary for the books I had illustrated. If I found it difficult to switch off to cheap production I do not blame the private presses— quite the reverse—for in the problems of the fine book lay the foundation of all my future work. I had learned that quality of work had nothing to do with the fee that one was paid or the cost of the book. I had helped to make books because they were worth making.

I have to thank Blackwell for his enterprise in trusting me with such important productions when I was completely unknown and inexperienced, and for the knowledge that I acquired from him and Newdigate. But for these men I may have dropped illustration for lack of a job; instead, I was given an exacting apprenticeship that forms the basis of my outlook on books and engraving to the present day.

Note. The line blocks made from old magazines and books are faulty for two reasons. Firstly, because enlargement tends to coarsen, and secondly, because the originals are faded and sometimes badly printed. Nevertheless I found it necessary to enlarge them to make my point clear; besides, their intrinsic beauty does not depend on slickness; it remains, even in a bad block.

P

CHAPTER VIII

THE BLACK GIRL

I HAVE to admit that the specimens of fine book work that I packed in my folio were useless as I trudged round the publishers' offices. I had no other specimens, for although I was evolving some ideas on book-wrappers and various experiments in scraper-board, I had not got so far as to produce specimens. There seemed no reason in production until some real job came along to give it a purpose: design, to me, must fuse into purpose in order to come to life.

A folio of fine book work and plenty of ideas were no good to the men who were too busy on their own problems to give the time necessary to visualizing the enthusiasms of yet one more artist looking for a job.

I remember some comments:

'You would be too expensive for us.'

This impression must have been created by Blackwell's magnificent productions.

'We don't want that sort of book.'

Apparently my talk of possible experiments in commercial production had not been noticed.

'I don't like the type used in this book.'

This being the only comment, I gathered that my illustrations had not been noticed.

My memory is a convenient blank when I try to think of the more discouraging comments; once more I wondered whether I was suited to illustration in general or whether I should have to wait until some private press found another Greek book that needed wood blocks.

Since it was obvious that the private press was doomed for a few years the idea was not too hopeful.

I must, with due respect to the publishing profession, admit that I went to few of the important houses—I did not know of them and apparently did not enquire my way about. Those I have worked for since are not guilty of what is, after all, almost excusable behaviour. It is expecting too much of a publisher that he should be able to visualize the potential qualities of all the work he sees as well as being a business man—or is it?

Just before I had come to a final conclusion as regards publishers, and while I was still able to put enthusiasm into my conversation about books, I was given an intro-duction to Garfield Howe, who was then running his own publishing house in Soho Square. He was interested and sympathetic to suggestion. Finally he said to me quite frankly, 'I do not know how your ideas will shape or whether they are practical for the commercial market, but I would like you to try out a wrapper'.

I revised my ideas on publishers and sat down to do my first wrapper—literally my first, since I had not made even a rough attempt at such a thing before. The design was made on scraper-board. I had already formed some definite theories about this medium that I still adhere to. Every medium has its own peculiar qualities—its existence can only be justified by this fact. Scraper-board, when used to imitate wood-engraving, is vulgar and pretentious; when its peculiar qualities are recog-nized it becomes an intriguing method of making a drawing.

Scraper-board is a clay-coated board that can be painted black to permit the scraping out of the drawing to appear as white. It is thus it lends itself to imitation wood-engraving. In actual fact such imitation is only achieved by considerable skill and conscious effort— similar to the skill of the engravers of the nineteenth century, who imitated pen lines in engraved wood. The absurdity of this reversal of follies has not yet been fully realized. Whenever I have been asked to imitate a wood-engraving in scraper-board I have explained that I can engrave a block as quickly as I can imitate one. If scraper-board is to be used it should be used with freedom, and there is plenty of scope for freedom and invention in this medium.

Black lines, and white equally, can be drawn easily and fluently, a thing not possible in wood; while a combination of specially prepared tints gives the designer a range of tones that will work into any design.

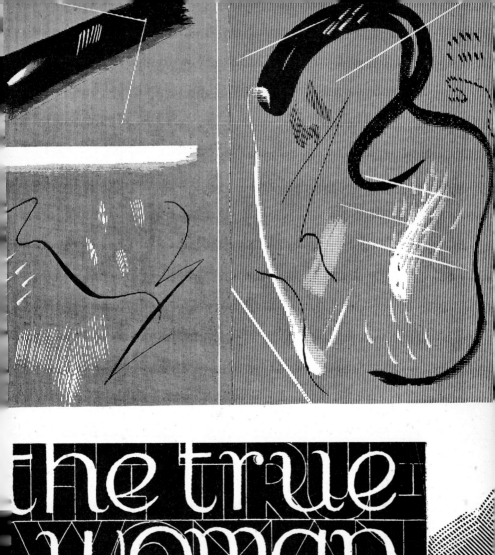

the true woman

Howe was pleased, and gave me several more wrappers, which enabled me to shelve that embarrassing question: 'Shall I abandon illustration and leave the publishing world to its own inertia, or shall I try yet a few more calls?'

I have always admired the artist who has such conviction that he can make up his mind to abandon art and take up farming, or, on the other hand, decide he is a certain type of artist and continue in that groove without question. I have that weakness in me that prevents me from wishing to repeat the past, even when such repetition may bring financial gain. Yet who would not wish to experiment when there are so many exciting materials to play with?—who is there that would make the same mental and technical approach to Homer, Samuel Butler, gardening books, books on birds and books on ghosts? And when all these books may be done in wood, metal, lithography, line-block, halftone—who would not draw, use the camera, paint in mud if necessary? as a very eminent painter once said in quite violent terms.

For the moment I have nothing to say about book-wrappers, except that the few I made for Howe carried me over to 8th May 1932, when I received a letter from Bernard Shaw, as follows:

Whitehall Court
8th May 1932

Dear Sir,

As I am old and out of date I have not the privilege of knowing you or your work. But Mr. William Maxwell, of Clark's of Edinburgh, tells me that you can design, draw, and engrave pictures as parts of a printed book, which, you will understand, is something more than making a picture and sticking it into a book as an 'illustration'. The idea is that you and I and Maxwell should co-operate in turning out a good-looking little volume consisting of the story contained in the enclosed proof sheets (please hold them as very private and confidential) and, say, a dozen pictures.

Are you sufficiently young and unknown to read the story and make one trial drawing for me for five guineas? That is, if the job interests you.

faithfully,

G. BERNARD SHAW

On the back of this letter was the following:

Suggested Subjects

1. *The Black Diana (not a Hottentot) going for Jehovah (as in Raphael's Ezekiel picture) with her knobkerry.*

2. *The same going for the god in Blake's Job.*

3. *The same accosting Koheleth, a very beautiful juvenile Plato.*

4. *The lion—'maneless', like Landseer's lions in Trafalgar Square. There used to be a delightful one named Dick in the Zoo who would let you handle him as in the story.*

5. *St. Peter carrying a full-sized Gothic cathedral on his shoulders, with the black girl rushing to help him (rather like Blake's little boy rushing after a butterfly).*

6. *Sundry faces from the Caravan of the Curious, like the Vanity Fair jury in the* Pilgrim's Progress—*if you have a weakness for the ugly-grotesque.*

7. *The black girl and Christ at the well: proffering the cup. Christ poor and humble, but unaffected and kindly.*

8. *Christ posing on the cross for sixpence an hour with the image maker (say yourself) at work, and Mahomet, very handsome, looking on.*

9. *The black girl and Mahomet scrutinizing a miniature Venus of Milo (no bigger than a big hourglass).*

10. *Voltaire (after Houdon) digging, with the girl looking at him over the garden gate.*

11. *The Irishman's dash for liberty: V. and the girl pursuing.*

12. *Family piece. The girl with all her children at home, with the Irishman digging, visible through the open door.*

It happened that the first thing I drew out of the letter was a cheque signed by G. B. S. That Bernard Shaw owed me five guineas was fantastic, but the idea of a hoax went out of my mind as I read the letter and scanned the proofs. It was not necessary to read the proofs carefully in order to realize that here was a great chance for illustration: the suggestions in Shaw's letter were evidence enough. With unerring skill he had painted word pictures that would stimulate the excitement of any illustrator, and the same skill had, in this one introductory letter, made the whole job so clear that I was able to begin work without any further discussion.

Shaw had picked the incidents with a good eye to their sequence; although, subsequently, more blocks were added to this original twelve, they were only embellishments to what was already an excellent and complete theme. In one sense, of course, it was a simpler task than selecting the drawings for a novel, since the episodic nature of the black girl's adventures gave the designs an individual character; their sequence was not a slow-moving one. Nevertheless, the situation was unique; an author had visualized his book as a series of pictures, and that very important first problem of the illustrator was done for me.

All that was left me was to select which of the twelve I should make my trial effort, and much depended on this selection. It was not only a question of getting a job of work, nor even of this particular job for an author so famous as Shaw with the possibility of its attendant publicity: any such gambling with the future is contrary to the practical side of an artist who knows that a job is only done by the effort of the moment. For one reading of the proofs had made me realize that, whatever some critics may have since said to the contrary, here was a small masterpiece as good as Voltaire's *Candide* and as seductive to the palette of an illustrator as any book could be. It was a book worth doing, and its contemporary flavour was refreshing to me after the years of delving into the remoteness of the Greek legends.

I chose the design of the artist modelling at his booth, perhaps, since Shaw had suggested using myself, because the model was immediately accessible. I felt rather as I felt when I started on my first book for Gibbings—just as one always feels at the first moment of a new job.

Trial engraving made for the 'Black Girl'

This first effort is the most difficult, when the illustrator is not warmed up to the job or grown into his part just as an actor must do.

Many roughs have been turned down because it has not been understood sufficiently that an artist needs time to work himself into a job before he reaches his zenith of achievement. With the best will in the world no artist can do himself full justice in a trial drawing or rough. Thus, with this knowledge, my anxiety was increased. I feared that Shaw, with his familiarity with artists of considerable reputation, would expect a higher standard than I was able to achieve in my first effort.

In spite of all anxiety the block was engraved and pasted in position with a few pencil roughs showing the possibilities of other designs.

The reply came back as quickly as an answer was possible by post. It is dated 24th May. My drawings were sent off on 22nd May, which shows that I had spent two weeks in evolving the first engraving and sketches.

Whitehall Court

24th May 1932

Dear Mr. Farleigh,

Good: I think you can make a real job of it. I want the book to fit into my standard edition; and when I return to London on Sunday I will send you one of the volumes, though we shall probably have to use a thicker paper as the story is so short. The print will be as in the proofs.

And now, business. I shall want the right to reproduce all over the globe during the whole term of copyright as illustrations to the book* *for a lump sum, payable in such advances as you may need, and the balance on completion. You must give me an outside estimate, as I have to calculate what I can afford to sink in the book. The estimate can be either for the whole job or per page illustrated. You must give me a date for completion. This is the most irksome part of the affair; but it's got to be done. So sit down and get it over.*

The Germans are pressing me hard to let them have a German illustrator, especially one who has been imprisoned for blasphemy, and richly deserved it for his hideously clever work. We must show them how it should really be done.

faithfully,

G. BERNARD SHAW

**You need not assign your copyright to me. You can license me to reproduce, and retain your right to reproduce, exhibit, and sell the pictures as drawings apart from my story if you have occasion to do so.*

This letter, as concise as the first, covered the second stage of the job as completely. I answered it and received a postcard reply.

Whitehall Court
27th May 1932

That is all right, of course; so go ahead. I am just off to Oxford for a few days and will put the affair into proper shape when I return.   G. B. S.

I rested for a while after this effort, and began to collect the material and make the plans that would carry me through the job. I met William Maxwell, of R. and R. Clark, Edinburgh, who was to print the book. After

a little banter, which I have since discovered is as peculiar
to Maxwell as it is Scotch, we arranged that a council
of war should be held after I had met Shaw and discovered his ideas about production.

A telegram arrived:

10th June 1932

Will you lunch with me at Whitehall Court to-morrow 1.15
to discuss page and print?

BERNARD SHAW

Once more concise, 'to discuss page and print'. Does
Shaw never get his ideas mixed nor express himself in
anything but the correct phrase, I wonder!

I reached Trafalgar Square fifteen minutes too early
and sat on a coping of the fountain looking at the lions
that had been mentioned in the first letter and wondered
what the next few hours would be like. I had read Shaw,
seen his plays, and worshipped him from afar, but had
never actually seen him. The accumulative effect of the
book, his letters, seeing him for the first time, as well as
talking to him, was enough to keep my mind occupied
for that few moments of killing time.

Then I found myself talking to Mrs. Shaw in a room
that seemed to look over the whole of the Thames—
such vistas were consistent with my state of mind, a
state that might have resulted in a vertigo but for the
skill of Mrs. Shaw.

A tall figure entered—strange and unreal this play: or
is it life that is so theatrical? I was sitting at lunch ex-
changing ideas on painting, sculpture, architecture, and
hearing talk of Ruskin, Morris, Lethaby, the Arts and
Crafts Movement, and discussing the fate of Waterloo
Bridge. Shaw did not mind if the present bridge was

removed since he could see more of the river beyond if it were better designed. Mrs. Shaw liked the old bridge—what did I think? What could I say, for while I could see the argument from both sides I was most concerned over the problem of the book I was there to discuss. Time was passing—so much had been talked of, but no mention of The Book. It was only afterwards that I realized the skill of my host and hostess, who had, by their conversation, established a friendly and conversational footing that made the subsequent discussion of work a simple affair.

2.45. Shaw produced some alternative pages of type and asked which I preferred.

Myself: 'I prefer the page that I have already worked to since I have visualized the book in that form now, and scaled my engraving to the type.'

Shaw: 'But a more open page will make the book thicker—a thing every publisher and bookseller wants.'

Myself: 'I would rather make it a thin book. It will be worth having, even as a thin book. Incidentally, I wish to remove headlines.'

Shaw: 'But people will not know what book they are reading.'

Myself: 'They'll know all right, without being reminded on every page.'

Shaw: 'Look here! Do it yourself.'

With this remark the proofs were handed over and the clock showed that barely fifteen minutes had passed.

I was walking back past the lion, who looked even more friendly. Illustrations and pages of type were going through my mind mixed up with the impressions of the past two hours, and, peeping out of all this in a curiously persistent way, was a small carved 'totem' of Shaw that had engaged my attention while I had been talking to him. It seemed curiously clear when every other impression was so confused; perhaps I could put it into the book somewhere.

Back in Hampstead I wrote to Maxwell for galley proofs. I intended my designs to merge into the text; to come into direct contact with the actual paragraph that was to be illustrated. The illustrations were to flow into the text and read on with it. Captions were to go the way of headlines.

Galley proofs were necessary since I must cut up the text, page by page, to discover where my drawings could start and how many lines they would occupy. In this way the text itself was responsible for the placing of the blocks, and often the size of them. Here and there I was able to enlarge or reduce by a few lines; sometimes during the later stages of pasting up an adjustment from the beginning was necessary. A certain freedom was left in which to make a few of the more important designs full-page.

As I cut the galley proofs I made sketches en route, and in a short time I had all my spaces worked out into which I could fit the blocks. This stage is not an easy one, since type is not elastic; sometimes a block had to go on the page opposite its context—it is not always possible to make the block flow into the text, as I had intended it should.

This book you are reading was made in the same way. The illustrations were not arranged or drawn until the galleys were cut up and pasted in position. This method ensures the text and illustration marrying as closely as is possible.

Maxwell wrote me that Shaw had said I was to engrave my own title-page; I made a rough sketch in pencil showing the Black Girl wandering through tropical foliage among which could be seen images of different gods, one of which was the 'totem' of Shaw that I had seen at his flat.

The sketch was sent to Shaw with a request for the 'totem' to be sent me that I might make a careful study of it. The drawing was returned with the following comments on the back:

15th June 1932

This is all right as a design. But the girl looks a bit wooden and tubby. I enclose a classical design which goes to the other extreme. Try striking an average.

Excuse my draughtsmanship.

I send the totem—a better one than the mask at Whitehall Court—by this post.   G. B. S.

??? You might bung in the lion looking over her hip.

This drawing was the first of a series Shaw was to make for this job, and they contributed not a little to the careful criticisms and suggestions that he made. The visual power behind them is extraordinary: they contained everything that was necessary to make his point clear. This in itself was a good enough lesson for any illustrator. Clarity of purpose must overcome technical efficiency as well as technical difficulties. At a later stage of the book, when talking on the phone to Shaw, I told him that his drawing was improving so much

that he would not need me before long. He replied with a chuckle, 'I did not set out to be Shakespeare, but Michelangelo!'

Q

I believe he enjoyed making the drawings or he would have spared himself the extra effort at a time when he was not only studying and criticising my drawings very carefully, but was busily engaged in writing and rehearsing plays, as some of his letters show. And yet he succeeded in giving me the impression that he had plenty of time to give, and that this was the most important job in hand. It is a tribute to him that he could make me feel that this small book was so important to him, and that I was so important to it.

While I was making studies for the first illustrations I was trying to evolve a method of producing a drawing that Shaw could see before I made the final engraving. This was not easy, since I had not a clear idea as to how I would engrave it; except that I intended to break away from my previous book work and move in the direction that had been indicated in the print of 'Hemlock'.

This fact of having to find my way resulted in the drawings resembling the final engraving, which is not generally a wise plan, since it limits the type of drawing; the limitations of engraving being felt before the actual craft is reached. I believe now that the study for the engraving should be concerned mainly with the problems of true drawing—that is tone, character and form, and that the final engraving should be an effort to interpret the drawing, even if the engraver burst himself in straining the limitations of his craft. Only this way can engraving be called creative.

To make a drawing look like an engraving is almost as futile as to make an engraving look like a drawing: however, on this occasion it worked well enough.

As far as I can remember the first few drawings came

back with no comments, and I considered the advisability of working out a cover design; partly, I admit, because a suggestion had been made of using some decorated papers which I did not think would go well with the rest of the book. Working from the suggestion, however, I produced a decorated paper of my own and an alternative design of a large portrait of the Black Girl. On the back of this was a large spray of leaves.

I sent these sketches off, and Shaw replied:

Whitehall Court
6th July 1932

Dear Mr. Farleigh,

Yes: the portrait cover of course. What about the other for endpapers?

Just consider whether she is not—for so critical a god-seeker —a little too brutish. It is a quality that justifies itself completely on the purely artistic side; and I hesitate to suggest anything in the nature of a literary and intellectual irrelevance; but still, recollecting that Michelangelo placed himself at the head of all the artists by making all his subjects geniuses, I am not sure that the slightest gathering up of the corners of her mouth and squaring of the outside ridges of her brows would really damage her. I am a critic myself, and have that outside lift of my brows emphasized by what are almost secondary moustaches; and without them I should look as brainless as the Sistine Madonna. I enclose a couple of picture postcards to show what I mean.

As to headlines have it your own way; only do nothing for the sake of consistency alone: consistency is the enemy of enterprise just as symmetry is the enemy of art. I should have a different rule for every page if it were worth bothering to

that extent. Maxwell could not run his establishment without
rules, but we can do as we like, short of disgracing him with
his Guild.   *faithfully,*

G. BERNARD SHAW

Thus the endpapers came into being; the decorated
wrapper became the endpaper at Shaw's suggestion. [It
may be interesting to note here that the small unit was

engraved and printed in repeat. I sent the print off to
Maxwell to make his line-block from it. He returned it
with a letter to the effect that he was having no line-
blocks in a book of wood-engravings—would I please
engrave the whole block. As a result of this, I was able
to hide the joins that usually show on a repeat pattern.
A glance at the proof opposite will show that the joining
up of the small repeat unit is not easy to discover.] It
also appears from this letter that I was still struggling to
get rid of headlines—most likely trying to convince
publishers and printers that I was not insane and had,
apparently, drawn Shaw into the battle.

The sketches for the cover were returned to me.

Whitehall Court

13th July 1932

Dear Mr. Farleigh,

*Don't bother about me: it is your job; and being an artist
myself in my own line, I know better than to find a good man
and then interfere with him. The only thing I can suggest is
that the label on the cover need not be foursquare if it would
please your fancy to scroll it. I've stuck a bit of paper on to
show what I mean. But I am not clear as to whether this
admirable design (I did not spot the lovely black girl in it at
first) is now to be an endpaper with the big face as the picture
cover. Do not forget that there will presumably be a jacket
with a striking design. If so, I am for black and white, and
not for red and yellow. What about the big face for it?*

*I rather hanker after a picture of the Roman soldier on
guard beside the cross before the arrival of the black girl.
Instead of I.N.R.I., S.P.Q.R. And a bucketful of nails,*

scourges, thorn crowns, etc. The soldier, very imperial and imposing, might have his foot on a torn-up scroll with the inscription still legible on the four pieces. Judge not that ye be not judged. It would serve him right if a knobkerry, grasped in a black hand, appeared over his unconscious head like the sword of Damocles.

However, I repeat, let yourself rip, and do not let me hamper or distract you.

G. B. S.

Shaw appears to have forgotten the decision to use the large portrait, so I wrote making it clear that the design would be pasted on to the board covers, as I wished the portrait to be an integral part of the book: not thrown away as is the fate of most wrappers. This letter also shows the first request for an illustration additional to the twelve suggested in his first letter. This meant that my paste-up was rendered obsolete—at least the section of the book that came after this passage.

I sent off the drawing of the Roman soldier.

Dear John Farleigh,   18th July 1932

This chap is wrong: he is standing at ease and looking quite reassuring and good natured, which destroys all the symbolism. Besides, artistically he is secondhand: the Italian Renaissance pictures have that very soldier all over them.

My fellow should be rigid, straight, inhuman, threatening, ruthless, with a horrible sort of clean beauty and athletic training to emphasize his mechanical cruelty. You must straighten up his knees and square his shoulders and give him Egyptian breadth of chest and slimness of flank.

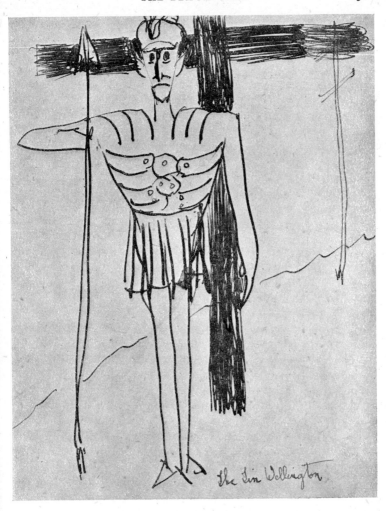

The Sir Wellington

*My own drawings, which I offer rather as a warning than
an example, suggest the pretentious futility of Cheltenham,
not the pride of Rome.*

ever,

G. B. S.

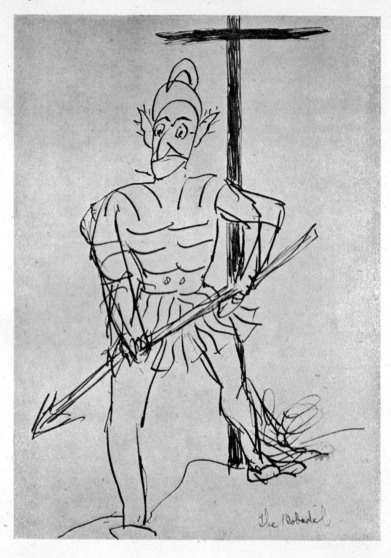

I don't dislike your soldier, all the same. He composes nicely; but he seems to see the joke.

The final drawing for the cover design was sent off, with a new drawing of the Roman soldier, and came back with a drawing which was the first that Shaw had made that was not based on one that I had submitted.

Whitehall Court

22nd July 1932

Dear John Farleigh,

As to the beanstalk I could only express the subject by a blatant comic cut, but as to the treatment it struck me that a repeated design like a miniature wall-paper, consisting of strips of beanstalk with lots of foliage and repetitions of a tiny professor clinging on between a pretty lizard-like crocodile and a dainty thread of a striking snake, might appeal to you as a pretty pattern suggested (to me) by the repetitions of the black girl in the endpaper, which are so very decorative.

The single beanstalk on an otherwise blank page looks a trifle bare and empty after the rich black front cover, and somehow the page does not make quite the right frame for it, though the leaves flow and hang very nicely.

The Calvary soldier is now perfect. Many thanks.

. . . .

. . . .

After this coming Sunday I shall be at the Malvern Hotel, Great Malvern, Worc.

ever,

G. B. S.

I made a new endpaper for the back of the cover which was based on Shaw's drawing, almost line for

Alternative
suggestion for
the Beanstalk.
Gives it a human
interest.

line; it seemed too good a drawing to be interfered with to any great extent. This was sent off to Malvern and returned with a small card:

Malvern Hotel

10th August 1932

With Bernard Shaw's compliments.

Just catching the post. Will write when you send the next batch.

The tree endpaper is perfect.

G. B. S.

It was some time before I had a sufficient batch of new drawings ready to send. The next letter from Shaw runs:

Malvern Hotel

25th August 1932

Dear John Farleigh,

Many apologies for my delay. I have been cobbling up my play, and could not get my mind on to the drawings in a properly leisurely way.

The lion and the Job are perfect. The other three need slight modifications. Ecclesiastes looks dead, like a figure in a frieze, because he is not looking at the girl. He also looks flat, like a profile cut in cardboard. All you have to do is to turn his head away from the spectator and towards the girl and all this will come right.

In the picture of the cathedrals you have produced an effect like Hogarth's Marvels of Perspective by not leaving a clear space between the girl's right hand and the tiny church in the distance. The result is that the girl seems to be carrying the church. Just shift the church up so that both it and the man's leg are clear of the girl's hand and arm and all will be well. You see, you cannot get aerial perspective in black-and-white, and are therefore dependent on scale and complete detachment.

Most important is the Christ. You have curiously reversed the relation between him and the girl. In the story he presents the cup to her; and he would obviously—since it is both a funny conjuring trick and an act of kindness—smile as he did it. But in the picture it is the girl who is the humorous conjurer with the kindly smile, and he who is accepting the cup; so you must contrive to turn the situation inside out.

The smiling Christ is a great chance for you. Most artists are so utterly floored by the problem of what Christ's face

ought to express that they just make it express nothing at all and cover up the failure with a sort of abstract holiness that makes him acutely dislikeable. The first painter who is sensible and human enough to paint a Suffer Little Children with Christ smiling at a child standing on his knee will

completely snuff out Holman Hunt's 'Light of the World'.
If you can paint in oils, here is your chance.

If you are not satisfied with the cover, try the effect of
making the breasts a little more virginal as they are so prettily
in the subject pictures. That is all I can suggest.

As to the book, clearly it should have the title JOB on it.
I shall be here for at least another fortnight.

ever,

G. BERNARD SHAW

The figure of Ecclesiastes *had* been taken from a
frieze! I had omitted to turn the head towards the Black
Girl—Shaw scored on this point, as he did on a good
many other occasions; in fact, I discovered I was learning
the business of illustration from the best master possible
—a producer of plays, as well as author of them.

His remark on aerial perspective in black-and-white
is not quite accurate except for broad solid work. An
engraving that indulges in subtle tones can suggest as
much aerial perspective as is necessary by tone values
alone. The drawing of the cathedrals, however, by
having a clear white background, did subject itself to
Shaw's criticism, and so I cleared the space as Shaw
suggested.

The problem of Christ and the cup was an interesting
one. I suggest that every illustrator should try to make
a drawing of one figure giving an object to another.
It is not easy, as I discovered, to convey which is the
giver and which the receiver.

The remark on the cover design refers to a letter of
mine which said that it was not entirely satisfactory. In

actual fact it was because the block was proving almost impossible to print. I had thought it a good block for Maxwell to experiment with; if he could print this block he would print the rest of the book. Maxwell was in despair at one stage and I was seriously considering re-engraving the whole of the cover design in order to get the fine lines and delicate stipple stronger and more deeply engraved. I thought it a good idea to let Maxwell exhaust every effort first before indicating that I would be prepared to re-engrave; he certainly spared no effort, and finally succeeded.

A meeting of Maxwell, paper-maker, ink-maker, machine man and myself, reached a conclusion that made it possible to achieve a successful result.

The reference to the Book of Job answers the query I made as to the title on the book held by the god (based on Blake) in the second illustration.

In the next batch of drawings to Shaw I included a revised version of the artist at his booth, the one that had been sent in the instance of his first letter to me. I was now dissatisfied with it, though Shaw had suggested leaving it just as it was. With the returned drawings he included a drawing of his own which was the first to be done in colour: it left me with the problem of showing a red beard through the medium of black-and-white.

His colour, like his drawings, was vigorous and direct in idea; these drawings are excellent examples of conceptive drawing, just as children's drawings are. This is not to say that Shaw's drawings are childish, far from it. That subtle quality of pure and unadulterated expression that so many artists are trying to recapture, perhaps not entirely mistakenly, from child art, is not peculiar to children's drawings; it exists in the mature work of art. It is, perhaps, best described as the triumph of pure feeling over the limitations of material. Children achieve this only from ignorance of their medium. It is their limitation also that they have little of importance to tell us—they have, after all, so little experience of life; but what they do say is said with a sweet clarity; this is their charm.

'The sky is full of flowers', says the child who has heard of, and seen, a garden, but not heard the word 'clouds' or seen that particular formation of clouds before.

Shaw's drawings are mature and highly skilful in thought and intention; their value to me lay in their intellectual clarity.

Malvern Hotel

29th August 1932

Dear John Farleigh,

You will see by the enclosed masterpiece what is wrong with the drawing of the flight of the labourer. My face is like the photographs they stick on to a ready-made body to amuse Bank Holiday trippers. Also it is drawn from one of the old photographs taken on ordinary plates without a colour filter, which represented me as a dark man instead of a very blond. The expression has not a trace of frantic terror, and the hat is an absurdity. The man is a very sophisticated metropolitan critic, and not a raw youthful labourer. Compare your own splendid portrait, full of dramatic energy and purpose, in the modeller's picture. However, you will see it all in my versions;

R

for though I am an execrable draughtsman I am a skilled and observant stage manager, always on the look-out for the right expression and movement. Keep me young, callow, fair, and scared out of my wits. Any photograph of a hurdle race will supply a study: I think he must have one leg over the gate: nothing else will give the necessary impression of headlong flight.

In the modelling picture, which is a triumphant improvement, keep Mahomet as handsome as you can: he was a princely genius. He is all right in the picture which shows him as discussing the Venus with the Black Girl. By the way, he abhorred images, and took the second commandment au pied de la lettre.

In the garden gate picture, if Voltaire had a small implement—a trowel or snipper or something—in his left hand, slightly raised, it would give him a perfect air of being taken by surprise in the act of gardening by the Black Girl's call. As it is, he looks as if they were old friends and had been talking there for years. Stage management again!

In the caravan picture the expression of the girl is lovely: and the Vanity Fair jurymen are all that could be desired; but the man with the moustache is very like some public man—I can't remember whom—but we may chance his taking proceedings.

I shall consider the wording of the colophon, and its form. I am inclined to describe the story as invented by me. Why shouldn't the pictures be drawn and cut in boxwood by you? On Friday I visited the Gregynog Press and saw some lovely wood-cutting work by Agnes Miller Parker. She blackens the block to begin with, and traces the design on the black with a red carbon paper. As the cuts leave the colour of the wood she

has the whole thing in black and white without having to
make trial impressions. Is this your way?

I am off to pay some country visits and shall not be back
here in Malvern until Wednesday.

ever

G. B. S.

The method of engraving referred to in this letter
was not the one I was using. I was making highly-
finished drawings that closely resembled the final
engraving. These were photographed on to the block
and so, by eliminating all intermediate stages between
the drawing and the engraving, I kept my interest fresh.

I always photograph a drawing on to the block if it
is elaborate in detail or is highly finished. I am thus left
free to interpret as I go and, as trial proofs are taken, the
ink can be removed easily from the surface of the block
without impairing the photographic image beneath.
Many engravers must have experienced the annoyance
of losing a drawing, that has been made in ink or paint,
while wiping the ink off the block during the process
of taking a trial proof.

If the drawing is an elaborate one the sensation is akin
to despair, for few artists can repeat a drawing that is lost.

I have a block that must belong to the nineteenth
century. It is prepared with a white ground, and on it is
a complicated pencil drawing of flowers, cherubs and
ornament. It is quite obvious that the engraver would
work from this block as it stands, for to ink it would
destroy the delicate pencil drawing. It seems that he
needed no device, such as 'inking-up' or filling his line

with chalk in order to see what he was doing. He knew what he was doing—so useful!

Voltaire, the labourer in flight, and Christ at the well, were revised and sent off—Shaw sent a card:

Malvern Hotel
7th September 1932

These are now perfect; but I want to suggest a trifling alteration in the silver cup one, and haven't time to do it before the post goes.

G. B. S.

The next day the drawings came back.

Malvern Hotel
8th September 1932

Dear John Farleigh,

The enclosed, just cut out of Punch, seems to give the correct position for a hurdle jumper's hind leg.

The well of Samaria makes a very nice picture; but somehow it does not tell the story; and I think that the sacred trinity of Holbein, Altdorfer, and Hogarth demands that the story should be told by the gesture. It still looks as if the cup were provided for public use (somebody having stolen the chain) and that the conjurer were taking it at the suggestion of the Black Girl, who is saying 'After you, please'.

The remedy is, I think, to lift the arm from the elbow or stretch it out from the shoulder and have the girl taking it with her right hand. This can be done without spoiling the composition. There is more life in the straight arm; but there may not be room for it. The proffering hand should be still proffering, though she has lifted the cup an inch or two off it.

By the way, since you draw cathedrals so featly, why not

*let yourself go on a regular holy grail of a cup? Pity there is
no use for a German fifteenth-century ciborium.*

That is all I can suggest.

*I have been heavily overdriven here for the last week or so.
I hope I have not hung you up by my delay in returning the
drawings.*

faithfully,

G. BERNARD SHAW

The drawing of Christ at the well was the most
troublesome of all in the book. I don't know whether

the action was difficult to convey, or whether I had been unnerved by the problem of the smiling Christ. However, Shaw finally wrote:

Malvern
12th September 1932

Dear John Farleigh,

That has done the trick perfectly.

I have to write a postscript to the tale, explaining its theology, but don't know yet whether it will invite illustration.

I return to London to-morrow.

I have lost count of the number of pictures; but I enclose £50 to go on with.

In haste, packing.

G. BERNARD SHAW

And so it seemed the book was finished. My paste-up was sent to Maxwell to await the go-ahead.

The suggestion of further illustrations to the postscript made me a little nervous that publication would be delayed beyond the Christmas market; neither was I anxious to rush work in at the last minute.

I sent my final account in to Shaw, who replied, as in all financial matters, very promptly.

Whitehall
24th September 1932

Dear John Farleigh,

Call it . . . in round figures, as there may be some odd jobs to be done in concert with Maxwell—perhaps even a drawing for the postscript if some very tempting subject cropped up.

I enclose a form of receipt (subject, of course, to your

approval), the effect of which will be that you retain your copyright subject only to a restraint on your sale of proofs until 30th June 1934. After that you can do what you like, except prevent me from using the illustrations as such: *that is, I cannot sell impressions apart from the book.*

I will tell Constable to send you 25 copies of the book for your private needs. As the published price will be half-a-crown only you may turn an honest penny by buying extra copies and selling them to collectors with your autograph at fantastic prices.

One fearful mistake has been discovered.

Aircraftman Shaw, alias Colonel Lawrence, Prince of Damascus, etc., etc., who is among other things a keen book fancier, saw yesterday the set of proofs you sent me (many thanks) and highly approved of them, but made the devastating remark that no Arab ever sat with his legs crossed. We shall have to assume that Mahomet was an exception to all rules.

I have noticed in my travels that Moors and such like never look well when they modernize themselves by sitting in our fashion, and are extraordinarily dignified crosslegged.

I shall be at Ayot St. Lawrence, Welwyn, Herts, until Wednesday afternoon.

faithfully,

G. BERNARD SHAW

I mentioned this error in the pose of Mahomet at my first lunch with Shaw: it was the main point I made then for redrawing it. But Shaw, while agreeing that it was the wrong pose, felt that, on this occasion, it was a pity to alter a good design for the sake of an academic error, and that we were justified in pleasing ourselves. His letter suggests that he had forgotten this conversation, though he finishes up with a similar conclusion that Mahomet was an exception to all rules.

The 'proofs' he refers to were those I had sent to him as what I had imagined to be the complete job.

I imagine that during this next few weeks the printer and publisher were getting more and more impatient. There were still no signs of the postscript, and there was also the possible added delay if it were to have illustrations.

A few hopeful notices appeared in journals and newspapers to advertise the advent of the *Black Girl*, but, very cautiously, gave no date of publication.

A magazine—I forget its name—promptly wrote for permission to reproduce some of the illustrations. I referred this request to Shaw. The date of his reply will be noticed to be ominously late considering the usual Christmas book is on the market by then.

Whitehall

17th October 1932

Dear John Farleigh,

I don't think it would do any harm to print two or three of the pictures in the new monthly: quite the contrary. It would be an advertisement.

But on going through the proofs sent me by Maxwell I don't feel that the story is illustrated enough. It needs two more pictures: Pavlov sitting on the crocodile, and Micah, with a flame shooting from his roaring mouth, and the Black Girl and the lion flying for their lives in divers directions.

*If it would amuse you to do these I will spree another
. . . guineas.*

What do you think about it?

ever

G. BERNARD SHAW

It appears from this letter that Maxwell had set the
book up according to my paste-up and sent it to Shaw.
The drawing of Pavlov was in colour and was Shaw's
own composition—I followed it quite closely in my
final version.

In spite of the delay that two more drawings entailed,
I was pleased to get back on to the job I had thought was
finished: I was realizing that I was going to feel quite
lonely when the *Black Girl* was finished; so, nothing
loth, I sent off to Maxwell for my paste-up. This had
already suffered badly from revisions owing to the
extra designs that had been put in. It was now in a
precarious condition and needed the utmost care in
taking to pieces again. For over a day I wrestled with
the worn-out pages, trying to find out what spaces I
could allow for the new blocks without destroying my
existing arrangement. Finally I got the pages right except
for the last two, and these I abandoned, for the moment,
in complete despair.

The new drawings were made and sent off, and a
postcard came back:

Welwyn

26th October 1932

*I have only just received Micah and Pavlov, too late to deal
with them to-day; so Maxwell must wait.*

Make a note to address letters as above for delivery on Saturday afternoons to Wednesday afternoons. Thursday to Saturday mornings, Whitehall Court. Otherwise there is a day's delay, as they have to be forwarded.

                                            G. B. S.

Another postcard followed and proofs of the postscript with two drawings by Shaw—suggestions for illustrations to the postscript.

Still life, with Typewriter, to recall the reader to modernity and a stuffy study from the forest and the garden

                                Welwyn
                        30th October 1932

It is Sunday; and the letter containing the Micah design will not fit into the receptacle of the closed post office.

In the cross headings for the preface, if you like still life you can put in anything of a literary nature except an ink-stand, which won't go with a typewriter. Extra books can

be Writing Made Easy; How to Spell; *and/or Inge's* Outspoken Essays. *If you prefer animals you can fill the grass round the B. G. with them.*

G. B. S.

I did not put *How to Spell* on one of the books, but I made a serious spelling error. In the first edition Genesis appeared as Genises. I altered the block in a later edition at Shaw's request, as the new spelling of the word was assumed to be his innovation, and he warned me, over the 'phone, of the threat to his correspondence on this matter.

The next day the drawings of Micah and Pavlov came back with a postcard enclosed:

Welwyn

31st October 1932

I think the carrion bird was a mistake of mine. It destroys the sense of space in the sky instead of suggesting it.

In my sketch, which was too sketchy to be clear, the professor had his hands folded on his left knee and his right knee swinging over them. This would pull the arms straight and take away from the stockiness of the figure: but it would give

an unaccountable silliness to him which might be worth it.
Just draw two or three lines and see whether it would be
any use.
   Otherwise O.K.   G. B. S.

In my drawing I had left out the carrion bird, suggesting to Shaw that the design would be better if it
were left out. On the back of the Micah drawing was
the following:

   This is too comic. The preface explains.
   The prophet seems to be swallowing a colossal banana
because the girl has not her fingers in her ears, and might be
running to post a letter. One must always connect the figures
by some gesture that knits the parts of the picture into a story.
   The lion is too obscene for so sublime a moment. He should
not be degraded *from the King Dick picture.*
                                             G. B. S.

I made a new drawing of Micah based on Shaw's
drawing, and also revised my own design by altering
the flames, the lion, and by raising the hands of the Black
Girl to her ears. I indicated that I preferred my own
Micah and thought it would work out better as a design.
These came back with the remarks written on the
drawing.

   I also have a weakness for this Micah. But if you study his
wrinkles and nostrils you will see that they indicate a strong
biting action. If you can get the uplift into his eyes and mouth,
the substitution of the flames for the banana will make another
man of him.
                                               ever
                                            G. B. S.

I do not like the new lion—I never did like it. It is the only occasion when I gave in to Shaw to regret it. On all other points he either convinced me or I convinced him. But the lion I dislike.

A request for permission to show some of the engravings at, I believe, the Wood Engraving Society's Annual Show was answered by a card:

Welwyn
8th November 1932

I see no harm in exhibiting a selection: not, perhaps, the lot. If before publication, all the better.

G. B. S.

The sketches for the postscript were made in pencil—time was too short to make finished drawings. They were returned with approval, engraved, and sent off.

There was still the problem in the layout of the last two pages. Before the postscript was added I had intended the harp design to appear as a tailpiece. This had now to be shifted to the end of the book—in other words it became a tailpiece to the postscript. The script at the end of the story finished with only two or three lines of type on the last page. As the block was engraved there was nothing for it but to ask Shaw to write a few more lines. It was obviously easier to ask that than to ask him to leave out some of his story.

Shaw replied:

Welwyn
9th November 1932

Page 58 is horrid, I shall write in 20 lines to bring the letterpress over from p. 57 and shift the picture down to the base line.

The harp must come on p. 75 as a tailpiece.

Then I think the thing will be as good as we can get it.

G. B. S.

Shaw had co-operated so easily throughout the whole of the book that it was not until later that I realized both my temerity in asking him to write more story to fit into my designs, and his complaisance in doing so. The production of the book had seemed so essentially a job of work in which several of us were engaged, Shaw, Maxwell and myself (as Shaw had said in one of his early letters), that I saw no reason, at the time, for not putting my difficulty forward and suggesting the solution. Shaw must have felt the same as I did or he would not have added more text with such promptness.

At last I received a letter that proved beyond all doubt that our work was done.

Whitehall

13th November 1932

Dear John Farleigh,

At last the book has gone to press. It isn't half a bad job, is it? The girl makes a charming Leitmotif running through all the pictures. Anyhow, it's been a bit of fun.

Is the enclosed all right for the extra illustrations?

faithfully,

G. BERNARD SHAW

The only thing left was for Maxwell to send me proofs of the whole book set up according to my paste-up so that I could check the position of my blocks.

This last job of the illustrator is a most important one. No paste-up, however careful, is exact enough to show the printer the position of a block to a hair's breadth. The shifting up or down, to left or right, until the block

s

is perfectly placed, is the final touch that makes a page a good composition, or, as the printer would call it, a good 'layout'.

It is probable that Maxwell still possesses my paste-up —if it still holds together: it is covered with corrections and would make an interesting example of the gradual adjustment of the work of artist and printer to its final conclusion.

'Where do you want your block to go?' asked the printer.

'Where is your type going, and what space does it occupy?' is the reply of the illustrator.

The artist and printer are component parts in the design of a book. If the work of these two craftsmen is brought together only at the end of a job, it is like a marriage where the bride and groom have not met previous to the ceremony; it is successful only by accident.

The period of waiting, between the completion of the illustrations and the publication of the book, is often a long one. This knowledge usually relaxes the tension of the artist, who is waiting to see his work for the first time as a finished job—a thing he cannot do until the book is finally printed, just as an engraver is unable to see his print until the final proof is taken.

For this particular book there was no relaxing of the tension. It was being rushed off at full speed; 5th December being the date now fixed for publication.

I sent off the proofs to Shaw of the extra blocks to complete the set that I had previously sent when I had thought my job complete.

Whitehall

30th November 1932

Dear John Farleigh,

Many thanks for the proofs. Wilson (of Bumpus) might like the decorative design for an advertisement board in Oxford Street if the sale proves torrential. Even a sandwich man——!

By all means let . . . reproduce to illustrate a review. . . . They must wait for the 5th December before reviewing.

I shall look in at the . . . to-day if possible. When the question of reproduction arises with reference to the management of the publishing—to illustrate, for instance, you had better just refer the inquirers to Constable & Co. Newspapers and magazines are very touchy on the point of all having equal privileges, and any favours should be handed out impartially by the publishers. . . .

ever,

G. B. S.

P.S. Kyllmann (Constable) reports that the first edition of 25,000 is already sold to the booksellers. He adds 'Great excitement about John Farleigh'.

The decorative design Shaw referred to was one of my large annual engravings. When the illustrations for the book were finished I had thought it a pity to drop the acquaintance of the Black Girl; the motive was too good. And so a three-quarter length figure of her was engraved, pushing her way through tropical foliage, still searching. It was my first large block that had not been adapted from a painting, but that had sprung up as an independent idea suitable to the form of a decorative engraving. In fact, it began a series of imaginative designs on a large scale, some of which sprang from a book, as did the Black Girl, and the others quite independent of book or painting.

In this particular block I used the simplest of outlines and exploited the stipple effect for modelling the figure. This seemed to give the velvety quality of the skin more than any other texture—though I believe it is only successful on black people, the high lights on the forms being very soft and subdued in tone.

While we are waiting for December 5th I will run through some of the proofs of the blocks.

The following section shows progressive proofs and illustrates the development from the first trial proof to the finished block.

It is usual to engrave as much as is possible before clearing away waste wood. As soon as any doubt occurs about the tone values the block should be cleared. It will be seen by these progressions that the tone of the engraving is very different when the background is clear. This must be borne in mind from the beginning of the engraving or the work will be engraved too fine, as the tones look lighter while the block is solid.

Detail of Jehovah Engraving   *1st state*

Detail of Jehovah Engraving   *2nd state*

Detail of Jehovah Engraving   *3rd state*

Detail of Ecclesiastes Engraving   *1st state*

Detail of Ecclesiastes Engraving   *2nd state*

Detail of Ecclesiastes Engraving   *3rd state*

Artist's Booth   *1st state*

Artist's Booth   *2nd state*

Detail of Voltaire in Garden   *1st state*

Detail of Voltaire in Garden   *2nd state*

Detail of Voltaire in Garden   *3rd state*

Endpiece   *1st state*

Endpiece   *2nd state*

Twenty-five copies of the book arrived in advance, plus twenty-five extra that I had ordered. I sent all fifty off to friends to arrive on the date of publication—I had none left for myself—I decided I would purchase a few copies on Monday, 5th December.

5th December. I passed a newspaper placard announcing 'Bernard Shaw and the Bible'. I went into a shop at 10 o'clock to get some copies: there were none left! At mid-day I tried again without success. On Tuesday I heard rumours that copies were being sold at 10s., for the first edition had apparently sold out and the next one could not be ready until Wednesday. I discovered a small shop with a few honest copies left and so managed to save a few first editions for myself.

The second edition came out on Wednesday to be followed by the third on Friday — it makes a nice

little story from beginning to end—the romance of
a book.

In two weeks I had received sufficient offers of work
to keep me busy for two years. Letters poured in; while
the press poured out lavish praise. Cuttings from the
press of the whole world are pasted in two volumes.
After that I abandoned the task of collecting press
opinions. I know well enough whether my work is
good or bad and do not wish to see indiscriminate
praise any longer.

'She was attractive'

'alluring'

'pleasing'

and all the rest of the adjectives, including

'delightful, but why nude?'

'embellished with exquisite engravings which depict
a heroine remarkably bathykolpous and kallipygous'

'pretty little picture book'

18th December. 'Sixth Impression printing' (advert.
in the *Observer*).

February 1933. 'The pulpits of Liverpool and Man-
chester translate the *Black Girl* to their congregations.'

A psychological magazine reviews the book and finds
much sexual symbolism, especially in the last engraving.
'We wonder if Mr. Farleigh was aware of this.'

24th February. America announces the publication of
an American edition.

I hope America will forgive me if I say that her edition of the book was a travesty of the English edition.

18th March. A letter sent to the press, signed as might be expected:

Sir,

I can understand the critics 'sitting' on Mr. Shaw for his recent book, but the way in which they have, with one exception, allowed Mr. Farleigh's drawings to go un-challenged is another example of that simple and press-like innocence, or is it ignorance, that newspaper critics adopt towards all illustrated books—unless for some reason an art critic is brought in.

Mr. Shaw shields himself behind his 'inspiration', and to do him justice he did not intend to be insolently irreverent. Mr. Farleigh was in no such mediumistic state when he illustrated the book, and is insolently irreverent whenever he is given the slightest chance. His conception of the Black Girl is physical rather than spiritual—she shows none of the tragedy of the black races, but more of the characteristics of an impertinent English girl who has been badly spoilt.

The Christ at the well is a dull Victorian conception, and the illustration showing the artist himself astride the cross, smoking a cigarette, is a clear indication of the artist's insolent attitude rather than the aloof one intended by the book.

I should be surprised if the illustrations have not done more harm than the text.

It is a pity the critics were not up to the other side of their job, when they could have harassed the artist as well as the author so that they might enjoy a well deserved burning together.

I am, etc.,

CRITICAL

The most gratifying review, next to this letter, was 'the pictures make the story clear to the blankest intelligence'; while the dizziest height of fame was reached when *Vogue*, in one of its reproductions of a fashionable woman, placed a copy of the book in her hand.

The book was denounced from the pulpit: it was purchased in a shop and publicly destroyed by a charming old lady.

But the birth-rate of Black Girls went up too fast for the destroyers: the machines poured out new impressions while the public went on buying.

Etc., etc., etc., etc., etc., etc., etc., etc., writes the press, who will never forget her.

Bless her! neither shall I forget her; but in writing her history, as an example of collaboration in the making of a book, I hope to lay her soul at rest. For I say now, once and for all, that I can never do *The Black Girl* again: I have no desire to do so—she belongs to the past.

Had I wished to, I could be doing her now—but she would have become old and withered and sad. I have done better work since—though not so popular. Perhaps one has to be much better to be as popular again; perhaps popularity is not, after all, a question of quality, but something that may happen at any time to anyone. It is a thought to console every struggling artist that a combination of circumstances may make him famous overnight. His struggle will then be one of preserving his integrity. It has taken me years to persuade publishers—the public is still unenlightened—that I am not an inveterate engraver, nor an authority on the tribes of Africa, but an ordinary artist anxious to experiment in any medium and on any subject.

In extenuation of all publishers I must record that Noel Carrington, of Country Life, has permitted me, when illustrating books for him, to work first, it is true, in wood, but secondly in pen, and thirdly in colour lithography; while future projects envisage the possibility of colour aquatint.

There seems no end to his appetite for experiment, to which he brings a sound business ability that will surely bring him to the front rank of publishers.

It is certain that English publishing owes much to such men, for in their hands lies the future of the English illustrator and the illustrated book. Without their support and encouragement a tradition that is peculiar to England would die from disuse.

Note. The drawings of Bernard Shaw reproduced in the chapter on 'The Black Girl' are the property of the Leicester Galleries and are reproduced by their special permission.

Elliot & Fry

Photograph by Paul Shillabeer. 1932

CHAPTER IX

BOOK-JACKETS

I N the two years that followed Shaw's book I made so many book-jackets that I have been tempted to insert here a section to discuss them, and their making.

The few that I had already made for Garfield Howe had shown me that the book-jacket provided plenty of scope for experiment, much more so than the illustration of a book. Where it is possible to be playful with a title-page, such playfulness throughout the book would be disastrous. How much more playful then can one be in a wrapper that is not only detached from the book but has, also, a life that is often momentary, or at best a few thumbmarked days!

The fact is that the wrapper has become more than protection: it is now decoration and advertisement, and is functioning most whilst the book is in the shop window and on the counter. If it looks well on our bookshelves, or lying on the table in our living room, so much the better; but the shop window has the prior claim.

The Victorian decorated binding has gone, alas! These bindings were designed to be held in the hand and felt with the finger tips. They were at one with the intricate patterns on wallpapers and textiles, and with the decorated waistcoat and the patterned flowers that were cultured then with such loving care. These books, that were clad so becomingly as to outer garments, are evidence that the men who considered the pages of the book, collected them together and illustrated them, also

T

thought them worthy of a suitable and permanent covering. And so they enshrined their labour in decorated bindings that were often exquisite.

Enough time has elapsed for the collectors to begin to cherish them. Such tardy recognition would be fatal to the bindings of to-day—if, indeed, they are ever collected—whilst the collector of book-jackets must be swift indeed if he would preserve a specimen before it is ruined.

The modern binding, or 'case' as it is appropriately called, is, no doubt, a remarkable thing in its way. When we have watched the machine slap the linen on to the board, and the finished case on to the book, and, rather absentmindedly, stamp a design on the spine, we are tempted to admire the smartness and efficiency of the process and its result. The truth is, there is not much wrong with the process or the organization of the machinery. Neither can these things be blamed for the production of shoddy designs. I think it is time the artist started getting curious—the machine cannot work well without him—and started designing bindings once more.

There has been some effort to make what is called a 'decorated' spine. It is a pathetic comment, and implies the previous baldness of books. So the spine is decorated! We are such bookworms, it appears, that we scan our shelves for a title and forthwith bury our nose in the book with no further concern for its appearance.

Or, does the decorated spine suggest that we like our books to look nice on the shelves, and, since they will never be disturbed again, the spine alone needs embellishment—like the bust of a Psyche in her niche, who dares not turn to look after us lest some inquisitive person should see her back and the hollow, tattered surfaces of her incompleteness. We must hide that which we have no wish should be seen, and our books creep away into their wrappers at the moment of their birth.

Their plain linen cases, especially when they affect the pastel shades, must be well protected; for, oddly enough, these cheap substitutes are more easily soiled and must, therefore, be more carefully protected than the well-bound book.

And the dust wrapper has slowly become more important: the artist has discovered a new field for experiment, while the publisher has realized the display value of this new activity. So the glory that was once the binding is now the wrapper.

So great is the temptation to make beautiful wrappers, for the artist must pour out his best even when the object of his attention is ephemeral, that it is more necessary for me to explain the limitations in designing wrappers than to enlarge on their possibilities.

The basic principles of wrapper designing may seem dull and restricting, but, as all working rules are capable of infinite embellishment, so the designer of book-jackets can please himself; just as the medieval carver must have pleased himself when once the structural principles had been accepted.

It is interesting to note that publishers themselves have shown a desire to make wrappers more attractive by sacrificing advertising space. The inside flaps are now used for price and 'blurb' that at one time appeared on the front cover; the back is often left comparatively free; while the entire wrapper, back, front and spine, is handed over to the artist, who is prepared to carry out his design in wood or lithography. This gift of space is no mean sacrifice on the part of the publisher, when we think of the fabulous sums paid for 'space' nowadays for advertising purposes.

Can we conclude, then, that the artists have, by making wrappers more and more attractive, seduced the publishers into a fondness for what must often be an undesirable extra expense? Perhaps, too, competition has made it necessary that wrappers should be given more and more individuality; and where should this individuality come from but the artist? Well might it be called an artists' 'racket'.

The skeleton structure of all wrappers is

The dotted line indicates:
  (a) top and bottom for trim off;
  (b) sides for turning over edges of book.

The drawing or colour should, if possible, fill this extra space to ensure:

(*a*) clean trim off top and bottom;

(*b*) design wrapping well over the edges of binding.

The dimensions should be obtained from a dummy of the actual book, which is provided by the publisher: the spine measurement is not the thickness of the book, since even a false spine is rounded in imitation of a real binding.

The simplest way to find the east to west measurement is to wrap a strip of paper round the dummy and mark the edges of the binding.

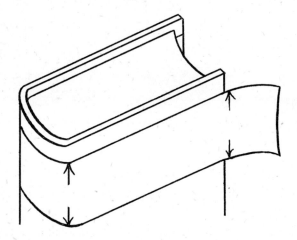

The design seldom spreads on to the back of the wrapper.

Reasons:

(i) Cost of process blocks often prohibitive;

(ii) Value of back for other advertising matter.

DISPOSITION OF LETTERING

This is almost as rigid in its arrangement as the alphabet, and, at first sight, might well dismay the designer who is anxious to create new arrangements.

This arrangement, for practical reasons of display, can seldom be altered or improved upon. Occasionally a title will run down the spine when a book is thin and the title long.

These diagrams show the key position only. I make no attempt here to suggest how the lettering can be absorbed into the general design either by sloping, curving, or otherwise merged by asymmetrical arrangement.

And now it is important to point out, in spite of what I have written of the weakness of the publisher for an attractive wrapper, that the lettering, especially the title, cannot be too legible. There is hardly a publisher who would not prefer a straightforward typographic design to any gilded beauty the artist may produce if the lettering is illegible. He will say, quite frankly, 'I am not interested in the artist so much as the book and the author'.

It is safe to assume that the maximum space should be given over to the titling, but against that we must put the fact that legibility is not always a question of size, as any good letterer will know. Again, a good designer will economize in space by flowing his illustration under and beyond the lettering.

It must be obvious to those who have read these initial stages of wrapper design that the business of lettering plays a very important part in the design. I would like to suggest that it cannot be made *too* important a part. The artist who dislikes lettering and is not prepared to make himself interested and become a master at it had best abandon the idea of designing wrappers, for the days are gone, or nearly gone, when an artist made his drawing and then abandoned it to some art director who arranged the lettering and general layout of the wrapper. It is left to the commercial studio to carry on this tradition; where the need for slickness and finish is greater than the desire for harmony between the drawing and the lettering.

While thinking that good finish is essential to good lettering, I would suggest that good balance with the rest of the design is preferable to perfect finish: neither good design nor legibility depend on perfect finish. This must not be thought to excuse bad workmanship: it is merely a warning. After all, it might be argued that good finish assists both legibility and design—it does on the whole, but I must point out that both of these qualities have been achieved without the perfect finish that we have come to associate with machine production. While it is true that every artist will approach his problems in his own way, it is possible to classify roughly as follows:

(*a*) The letterer who is highly specialized and makes good use of traditional forms—that is to say, he gives them a contemporary quality. The gravestones of the seventeenth and eighteenth century show that the masons were working with a full appreciation of beautiful letter forms.

(*b*) The letterer who has no knowledge of traditional letter forms, and produces bastard forms as a result of emulating that which is modish. The commercial studios are full of these men, though it is becoming increasingly evident that without proper training there can be no creative designers. The gravestones of the late nineteenth and early twentieth century reflect the tendency of that period to lose sight of good forms in the process of modernizing.

Note: Both (*a*) and (*b*) achieve perfect finish as a result of continuous practice.

Note again: That constant practice will also give freedom and invention to (*a*), while (*b*) will only become more slick and rigid. Thus the creative letterer will appear to be less highly finished, though the discerning critic will know that this freedom is the higher achievement.

And so, as I said before, neither good design nor legibility depends on perfect finish.

(c) The artist who does lettering occasionally and, while not achieving the same proficiency as the specialist, becomes a good creative letterer by his understanding of form acquired in his practice of designing for other purposes and his interest in letter forms. The best of our book-jacket artists belong to this category.

(d) The artist who is temperamentally incapable of the application necessary either to the study or practice of lettering, but produces a sketchy, dashed-off type of lettering that is nevertheless suited to his drawing. This method has the advantage of being as personal a statement as the artist's signature. I have seen an excellent wrapper designed by Vanessa Bell, the lettering of which would be condemned by any professional letterer, but which had character and a personal feeling that married harmoniously with the rest of the design.

Note: (d) as a class is more rare than (c).

Note again: The character of lettering produced by (d) can also be produced by (c) for, as I have said, good letters are not always highly finished. Perhaps one might say that (c) produces both classic and romantic lettering, while (d) produces only romantic.

It is not my intention to discuss the craft of lettering or the origin of letter forms. That has been done most adequately by Edward Johnston; while many books must exist that deal with the so-called 'Modern' letter forms.

I have written so much about lettering with the intention of making the prospective designer of book-jackets appreciate its importance.

The fascination of lettering, with all its ramifications, must be left to the individual to discover. For myself, I find an increasing amount of space is being occupied by those books, both old and new, that contain drawn or typographic title-pages—while the old songbook covers show as much variety as any form of publication both in medium and subject—a variety that seems to have inspired the designers to extraordinary degrees of whimsicality.

These covers are the forerunners of the modern book-jacket, though they are not free from the book, but form an integral part of it. Perhaps the modern magazine may more rightly claim the songbook cover as a parent— if so there is a sad falling-off—and I dare not say what I think of modern songbook covers.

A knowledge of period lettering, that can only be gained by browsing among old books, is as useful to the artist as a knowledge of period dress is to the designer of modern costume. Just as a dress designer will echo a period note in an ultra modern dress, so will the artist reflect the tendency of a period in the book he is decorating, both in the sense of detail and the general character of his lettering. There is a profound weakness in the artist who smothers his work indiscriminately with one style of lettering.

The opposite page shows a selection of six songbook covers of the nineteenth century and gives some idea of the variety of treatment that was so popular at that period.

I will leave the subject of lettering, in case it appears that there is no room left on the wrapper for the illustration, with the final suggestion that the wise designer

SUNNY WOODS

Melody by Tul.

GALOP.

12

Petites Fantaisies

DUBLIN. Dr MACKAY. ENGLISH CARTER.

SONGS BALLADS

WITH

PIANO-FORTE ACCOMPANIMENTS,

COMP... HARP,

A Canzonett,

VERDIS OPERA

IL TROVATORE "

will commence his design with the lettering, or introduce it at a very early stage of the first sketch. It is my own experience that to start with the illustration is to squeeze out the lettering. The ideal thing, of course, is to consider the illustration and lettering as integral parts of the design and draw them both together, just as a designer of a teapot must consider the handle and spout together with the body of the form.

THE MOTIVE FOR THE ILLUSTRATION

This should be chosen for its aptness in indicating the general character of the book rather than any one particular incident in the book. Some successful designs are made that would function equally well as illustrations inside the book, but they are exceptions to the rule that a wrapper should talk of the whole book and not just a part of it. I do not mean to insist that the design should be symbolic in an abstract way. Good realism can be as broad in its implication as any abstract design.

A careful reading of the whole book is necessary, though it will be found that the motive for the design will invariably be contained in the first half of the story. The design should have in it a certain prophetic quality— just as the author himself appears to have in the early stages of his book. There may be only a hint of the impending crisis in the first half of the book, and for the artist to ignore the final stages is to miss the true character of the story.

Most designers will discover that several alternative motives will appear, and one of these must be selected as being the most significant. Even if other interests are brought in, the one motive must predominate. It is obvious that the simple design will make the best wrapper, since it will have the necessary carrying value. But I must point out that by 'simple' I do not mean a circle or a cube: an elaborate design will achieve simplicity through its presentation. By simplicity I mean singleness of idea as against a confusion of conflicting ideas. This singleness of idea is no easy accomplishment: it is often wise to write the idea on the margin of the drawing and forget everything else.

Just as the title of the book is a symbol of its contents, so is the design on the wrapper; in fact the designer might confine himself to an illustration of that title, though I admit this is not always possible. When the artist has settled what he will do, he must prepare a 'rough' that will show the publisher exactly what he is to expect of the finished drawing.

It is necessary to have a knowledge of process reproduction or a suitable drawing cannot be made. Whole books have been written on the subject, the most recent being Harold Curwen's, and there is no excuse for the artist to be ignorant of these processes. This knowledge will not only make the artist's job simpler and give him the best results, but will stimulate him to a creativeness as a result of the limitations and variety of these processes.

It should be remembered that drawing for reproduction is not just a question of making an original drawing, any more than an engraver makes a drawing in imitation of his final engraving. Each process has its own peculiar quality which it imposes on the original drawing, and sometimes these qualities can be made part of the actual design.

The rough sketch should be made actual size. The finished drawing can be made any size according to the style of the artist. I work actual size for almost all jobs but pen drawings, as I prefer to design actual size; but it is not suitable to the temperament of all artists.

The term 'rough' is a technical one and does not mean rough; it only means that the drawing is not the final, finished drawing. The ideal 'rough' is one that requires very little work to make it into the finished drawing. Every problem of design, tone, colour and general treatment should be settled in the rough, else how is the publisher to judge if this is the wrapper he wants, or to know of its final effect? Even when the final version is clear in the artist's mind, he must be at pains to see that he makes it clear also in his rough. He should take no notice of the publisher who says he only wants a slight sketch, unless he has been working with him for so long that he knows and trusts his work implicitly.

To sum up, most of the work of the whole job is in the rough, and for this reason most artists, quite rightly, demand payment for roughs.

And while we make our rough, do we have a free hand in the design? Can we forget the public and what it likes? Are we allowed to forget the man in the street?

I have always thought it strange that the chocolate box tradition dies so hard a death in this modern world and appears even in a vague form in the publishing world. We all know that chocolate boxes must have an air of the harlot's boudoir about them; but why must book-wrappers be cheerful and pretty but never! oh, never! must they reveal the tragic side of a book? Is the

book-buying public to be ensnared by sugar and spice? I
am amazed that even a vestige of this tradition remains,
especially when it is common knowledge that a large
section of the public likes a good cry. Surely a consistent
note of charm must become suspect and finally boring.

Nevertheless, the rough is finished and sent in.

The artist is summoned to the publisher's office. The
author happens to be present.

Publisher: 'I am afraid this design is too gloomy; I
want the pastoral side of the book emphasized.'

Author: 'I think it is excellent—it is what I feel about
my book.' To the artist: 'What do you think?'

Artist: 'It is what I felt to be the significant note—a
motive that haunts it and is most moving.'

Publisher: 'But I can't sell the book with this wrapper;
you must try an alternative design.'

Later—publisher's office.

Publisher: 'This is a much better design and will sell
the book.'

Author: 'But it is not the important side of my book.
I like the first design and refuse to have this one.'

Publisher: 'Then what shall we do?'

Result: a plain lettering cover that annoys nobody,
neither does it really please anybody. Nevertheless it
was one of my best wrappers; but the book was too
good to be dismissed with lettering only. It haunts me
even now, and is one of the few that I wish to reread.
I do not blame the publisher—the chocolate box tradition was too insistent—it must go down as a minor
incident.

On one occasion I engraved a wrapper, the publication
of which sent me to a cocktail party in Chelsea. I came

away remembering none of the names of those who had been introduced to me. But two things stand out in my mind to this day: a young lady in superb and fashionably veiled hat embraced me metaphorically and said, 'Your design was just too gorgeous—I've just come from the theatrical garden party—so hot, you know—I did just love the Black Girl—just too thrilling. . . .'

And towards the end, as I was about to leave, a quietly and beautifully dressed woman, who might have been any age, asked me to sit down and explain my design to her. We talked for a while on many things— myself talking in sheer relief. There must have been many like her at that party, or was she, I wonder, the only real thing there?

This party, because it was coincident in time, reminds me of other visits to Chelsea to discuss with Cicely Hamilton the illustrations of some articles she was writing for *Time and Tide*. She lived in a small house that had all the air of the recluse about it. I always left it with a feeling that it was an oasis in a noisy and difficult world. I found it difficult to believe, when she sat opposite me in the quiet of her small house, that she wandered about the world and partook so actively of the difficulties and sufferings of mankind. In her place I would have seen few people and forgot the problems of social injustices.

Time and Tide were pleasant people to work for, though when I look back I dislike the work I did for them.

I was still interested in scraper-board and was making some rather unsuccessful experiments, while the slightly satirical, rather political nature of the illustrations for

Cicely Hamilton's articles were a little out of my depth. It was not that I was lacking in enthusiasm, for I found the political atmosphere of the *Time and Tide* offices very stimulating: I went to one of the staff lunches and enjoyed the mixture of politics and wit. Again I forget names, except that of Ellen Wilkinson, who arrived late and brought in a cool draught of determination and energy to what might have become too social a gathering. I believe Winifred Holtby was there, but I remember her better at some later date when I made a political cartoon for the paper.

Lady Rhondda, Winifred Holtby and myself discussed the subject of the cartoon, I admitting my complete ignorance of politics, while Winifred Holtby quickly and wittily outlined the situation of the moment and suggested ideas for my drawing. I went away with a more vivid impression of her than of the cartoon I was to make. Of that cartoon I can only remember inquiring, from some official source, as to whether I could put God and the King into my drawing. The reply was, 'Do what you like with God, but be careful what you do with the King'.

I am afraid political cartoons are not in my line, although I am occasionally incensed enough to wish I were a cartoonist.

Later, another magazine asked me to arrange and illustrate a four-page supplement of poetry. I sent in a typographic paste-up with blue pencil scribbles to show the position of designs. Before I put in more work I would settle the question of price. I was getting wiser!

The editor 'phoned she was delighted—would I meet

U

her to discuss 'details', an ominous term for 'price'? I sat in a well ordered modern office and asked forty guineas for eight blocks: five guineas per block, including arrangement of the supplement. The editor looked dubious and went to confer with a higher official, then returned.

Editor: 'We like your idea; it is exactly what we want, but we cannot spend so much money.'

Self: 'What do you wish to spend?'

Editor: 'About half that amount.'

Self: 'Very well! I will make another design with half the amount of decoration.'

Editor looks worried.

Self: 'What you want, I suppose, is this amount of work for half the price?'

Editor looks relieved.

I say I am very sorry and am a little bewildered, for the organization is a rich one. The editor goes for another conference and returns to tell me that the higher regions think John Farleigh is getting swollen-headed and demanding exorbitant fees! I suggest, with great restraint, that I can make no concessions, present the editor with my rough paste-up, as she is fond of it, to hand on to some unfortunate artist who is prepared to engrave eight blocks for twenty guineas.

Editor: 'Thank you so much! I suppose you couldn't suggest an artist who will do it for us?'

With still more restraint I refuse to suggest a good artist to work under such conditions, and returned home, having wasted the whole of a working afternoon.

Later came a 'phone call from the editor telling me, in great triumph, that she has got ———— to do the job.

A triumph, indeed, to take advantage of the shy nature of this particular artist. The next time I met her I gave her a severe talking to, but I doubt if she will ever have enough proper conceit to charge a price that is not seriously undercutting her fellow workers. Thus the menace of undercutting is not always of the unscrupulous: it is often the shy, charming natures that are imposed upon, as in this particular case.

The question of minimum prices has, since this incident, been agreed upon by the Society of Wood Engravers, and I insert them here for the benefit of all beginners with the hope that they will have the courage to stand for them, not only for their own sake, but their fellow artists as well.

'In order to avoid undercutting in prices and to form a basis for discussion with clients for the design, engraving and sale outright of blocks, the Society suggests that the following should be the minimum prices quoted by the artist:

Bookplate	5 guineas
Book-jacket	6 guineas
Poster	25 guineas
Window bill	12 guineas

'Illustration for Book or Advertisement:

Under 3″ × 2″	2 guineas
Under 3″ × 3″	3 guineas
Under 4″ × 3″	4 guineas
Under 5″ × 5″	7 guineas
Under 7″ × 6″	9 guineas '

to which I add minimum prices for drawn and litho book-jackets:

Drawn in line, $3\frac{1}{2}$ guineas.

Drawn in colour, 5 guineas.

Drawn in litho (one colour), 6 guineas.

Drawn in litho (two or three colours), 8 guineas.

Engraved in wood (two or three colours), 8 guineas.

These minimum prices should be asked by the beginner on his first commission. Beyond this the scale of prices must depend on the market value of the individual or on his own estimate of what his work is worth.

One wrapper that I made in 1933 deserves some comment. Faber's produced Cobbett's autobiography or, to give it its full title, *The Progress of a Ploughboy to a seat in Parliament as exemplified in the history of Wm. Cobbett, Member of Parliament for Oldham.* Cobbett left instructions, which were not carried out as far as I know, that this book should have on the title-page a portrait of himself as a ploughboy scaring the rooks from the field. This would be at the top, while at the bottom he was to be shown addressing the Speaker in the House of Commons.

I carried out this suggestion of one hundred years ago as a design for the wrapper. Since it was to be engraved the lengthy title was a formidable problem and needed some special treatment. I went to the British Museum and forged Cobbett's writing until I was passably good at it, and then wrote the title in his own hand, except for the simplification necessary to make it a legible title for a wrapper. Engraved as a white line on black it made a simple job out of what might have become over-elaborate and fussy.

Unfortunately, this wrapper was ruined by over-inking, a common fault in the printing of wood blocks.

Often enough a design will evolve this way. There are few dictates of author or publisher that are not capable of interesting handling—indeed, a good designer will often welcome such suggestions, since the varying nature of these demands often provokes a variety in design that might not come to the artist who is left entirely to his own devices.

A description of other book-jackets, if any others provoke comment, must appear in chronological order. I have said enough to include the main factors in the making of them, enough, I hope, to suggest that it is one of the most attractive jobs of the book illustrator. That there is infinite scope for experiment is as obvious as that the wrapper is quite peculiar as a problem for the designer.

I do not believe that wrapper designing is the job of a specialist, since I believe all specialization in so narrow a form to be a mistake. When an artist takes a drawing of a horse to Country Life, Carrington says to him, 'Can you draw a motor car?' He, too, is not in favour of specialization, and he is wise. Also it is fortunate for me, or he would never have commissioned me to illustrate some of his books that have given me as much pleasure as any that I have ever done.

The best wrappers have been made by illustrators who are designers in an even wider sphere than books: whose activities include painting, posters and several of the crafts such as etching, engraving and lithography.

And last, but not least, the wrapper is often the first job of the beginner, since a publisher will try out a new artist on a wrapper before commissioning a whole book. The prospective illustrator would be wise to include some specimens of wrappers in his folio on his first visit to a publisher's office.

I stumbled on wrappers partly by accident, Garfield Howe giving me my first chance before I was even certain of what could be done with them. I have made many and learnt much since then, but to this day I look on the making of a wrapper with the greatest of pleasure. I have not made one that has not afforded an opportunity for experiment, either in the drawing or the reproduction.

And, finally, may I put in the plea that artists and publishers combine to make the wrappers of the future comparable in quality and vitality to the music-book covers of the last century. The modern songbook cover is beyond redemption—nothing can save it now—but the book-jacket may yet achieve distinction.

CHAPTER X

ILLUSTRATING A BOOK

I HAVE said that every book is a different problem, and that the illustrator must learn his job afresh on every book. The purpose of the following section is to amplify this point. The illustrator who specializes in one type of drawing and one type of book learns his job early and need not concern himself with the rest of this book; for it will prove to him, probably to his disgust, that I have not yet learned my job.

Having no original intention of becoming a book illustrator myself, and not even to this day considering myself a professional, has probably prevented me (or saved me) from specializing. The list of books shown below, in chronological order, gives me plenty of material to draw from in considering the various problems in which the illustrator is likely to become involved.

Essays of Swift. Golden Cockerel Press, 1924; 12 wood-engravings.

Odes of Pindar. Shakespeare Head Press, 1928–9, 2 volumes; 88 wood-engravings.

Bede. Shakespeare Head Press, 1929; 4 wood-engravings.

Complete Homer. Shakespeare Head Press, 1929–32, 5 volumes; 51 full-page wood-engravings.

The Adventures of the Black Girl in her Search for God, by Bernard Shaw. Constable, 1932; 22 wood-engravings.

Little Arthur's History of the 20th Century, by Cicely Hamilton. Dent, 1933; 14 scraper-board illustrations.

Stories from the Bible, by Walter de la Mare. Faber & Faber, 1933; 9 full-page wood-engravings and 35 headings.

Short Stories, Scraps, and Shavings, by Bernard Shaw. Constable, 1933; 26 wood-engravings.

The Way of All Flesh, by Samuel Butler. Collins, 1934, 5s.; 14 wood-engravings.

The Story of David. A. & C. Black, 1934; 11 wood-engravings.

Bernard Shaw's Prefaces. Constable, 1934; title-page, wood-engraving.

Cape Farewell. Cresset Press, 1934; 8 pen drawings.

Three Fantastic Tales, by Claude Houghton. Joiner & Steele, 1934; 1 pen drawing.

The Precursors, by Cunliffe Owen. Athenæum Press, 1934; 3 wood-engravings.

Storm at Sea. Golden Cockerel Press, 1935; 4 wood-engravings.

The Man who Died, by D. H. Lawrence. Heinemann, 1935; 10 two-colour wood-engravings.

John the Baptist. Arthur Barker, 1935; 4 wood-engravings.

The Gods had Wings. Constable, 1935; 16 wood-engravings.

Hortensius, Friend of Nero. Lovat Dickson, 1936; 16 pen drawings.

A Country Garden, by Ethel Armitage. Country Life, 1936; 12 full-page wood-engravings, 12 headings, etc.

Plutarch's Lives. Penguin Books, 1937; 12 wood-engravings.

The Disappointed Lion, by Dr. Tucker. Country Life, 1937; 24 pen drawings.

This is the Way. Dent, 1937; 3 wood-engravings.

Back to Methuselah, by Bernard Shaw. Limited Editions Club, U.S.A., 1938; 25 wood-engravings.

Old Fashioned Flowers, by Sacheverell Sitwell. Country Life, 1939; 12 five-colour plates and 24 line drawings (litho and pen).

The dates shown are those of completion, and give no idea of the length of time spent on each book, some of which overlapped and fitted in with other jobs, thus often covering a period of several years, as in the case of *Methuselah* and the Sitwell flower book. Neither does the list include jobs other than those of illustrating books: these will be mentioned in their order, should any interesting detail occur to me as I write.

One interesting fact, shown by the list, is the relative proportion of engraving to other methods, wood-engraving predominating at the beginning.

I shall now consider each book in turn, in an attempt to summarize its problems. Swift, Pindar, Bede, *Homer* and the *Black Girl* have already been dealt with, and the last section, on Book-Jackets, brings me to 1933.

'LITTLE ARTHUR'S HISTORY OF ENGLAND'

The illustrations to this book were, with the exception of a few new drawings, those used for the weekly articles in *Time and Tide.* The wrapper design was made up from a paste-up medley of the illustrations made from printers' pulls and a photograph and reproduced combined line and halftone. The photograph, a back view of an Eton boy taken specially for the occasion, suggested Little Arthur contemplating the general effect of muddle. I have cut up proofs of illustrations to form an all-over pattern on many different occasions; the mixture of drawing and photography is now termed 'photo-montage' with the modern need to dignify a method of working with a descriptive label.

'STORIES FROM THE BIBLE' (1933)

was already published, but, as a considerable quantity remained in sheet form, it was proposed to reissue as an illustrated book. I was unable to inset my engravings, since the typescript was already printed, and so made full-page blocks that could be 'let in'. A small engraving was made for each heading, some thirty in all, and dropped into the existing space; this meant that the pages containing headings had to be reset and printed, but they gave the book a decorated quality where it might otherwise have appeared a makeshift job.

With some sketches I went to Taplow to talk with De la Mare—a few words with an author in the early stages will save more time later than can be estimated. My day at Taplow was a veritable feast of talk, though little was said about the book itself: a good author will explain his ideas in very few words. And yet the rest of the day's talk was more descriptive to me of De la Mare's ideas on his illustrations than the discussion of them in detail.

His is a delightful house with the true atmosphere of country living about it. Tasteful and sincere, it provided a delightful background to his conversation, that had, as well as these same qualities, a pervading sense of the mystic. But his mysticism is of a troubled kind: as if he were not quite sure of reality or fantasy. Every phrase, almost every word, he queries, and I found myself explaining so much to a man who was much wiser and richer in imagination than I was myself.

He seemed to find everything mysterious and worthy of his curiosity, and he probed in a charming and delicate, if troubled, manner. It is a subtle form of flattery in a host, though I do not think he meant it so.

Quite early in the day we were wandering round his garden discovering a mutual preference for flowers, cabbages and trees against the sunlight. Perhaps he finds more mystery when the forms of things are veiled with shadows and the light prinks out the edges of things, making patterns that are as subtle a quality as perfume.

I told him of my love of the 'Hemlock' and the print I had made of it, and his interest was such that I sent him a print on my return.

I left Taplow when the sun was sinking and the countryside was flooded with a warm glow; that same warm glow was in me as I looked back on my day with De la Mare.

> *Taplow*
> *June 8th, 1933*

Dear Farleigh,

We had friends with us up to yesterday evening or I should have written before this. I immensely enjoyed our talk, and look forward to your keeping your promise to come again.

The only drawing for the Stories I hesitated over was the Samson; but you very soon detected, no doubt, that I am a very amateurish appreciator. None the less, to 'know what one likes' doesn't imply any want of ardour in the liking.

Dick told me when I saw him that his only criticism of the jacket was that it might not attract the avuncular (or auntine) eye—but it doesn't say much for the eye.

I love the 'Hemlock', and can even catch some insight into the mastery of the workmanship. But you must tell me when we meet again a little more about the three aspects.

Yours sincerely,

W. J. DE LA MARE

P.S. *Would you let me have a postcard saying exactly how you think the engraving would be best framed?*

Taplow

14th June 1933

Dear Farleigh,

Many thanks for your letter, and do send me a word suggesting a day when you can come again. I shall look forward to another talk.

By 'a plain wood frame' I gather you mean not black. I want to get the beloved 'Hemlock' framed as soon as I can, so if I don't hear I will take it that you mean unstained wood.

Yours sincerely,

W. J. DE LA MARE

The next four weeks were spent in engraving the blocks.

Taplow

Dear Farleigh,   *13th July 1933*

This is only a word to say that we are looking forward to seeing you on Saturday. A friend, A. E. Johnson, who is a poet as well as a scholar, and is just back from America on a visit to his native land, is coming too. He too is looking forward to seeing the woodcuts.

Yours sincerely,

W. J. DE LA MARE

I was a little dashed to hear that another guest was expected—probably a little jealous, remembering my last visit, when I had De la Mare to myself for a whole day. But Mr. Johnson proved to be a better guest than myself—his conversation was restrained and full of quiet thought. In the evening we returned to London together and then he spoke more than he had the whole day in rhapsody of De la Mare.

He sent me a copy of W. H. Davies's *Later Days* with the inscription

To John Farleigh, recalling a very pleasant meeting at Walter De la Mare's, July 15th, 1933.

A. E. JOHNSON

See p. 28.

I quote page 28 from Davies's book:

'On one occasion De la Mare asked me how I wrote my poems. This being a plain and simple question I began in this way—"First, an idea comes to me." But I had no sooner said this than De la Mare asked quickly—"What do you mean by 'an idea comes to you'?".'

The reader can imagine what a day I had in explaining my own mental and technical processes to a mind that was so curious and probing.

There is little I can relate of the actual making of the illustrations. The Ark of the Covenant gave me some trouble. There is a description of it in the Bible, but it was too ambiguous without some kind of pictorial representation, and this I was unable to obtain, though I wrote to Palestine. Finally I tracked it down in an old concordance—small and dull as a drawing, but enough to clarify the description sufficiently for my purpose.

I regret that the full-page blocks were ruined in the printing—again they were overinked.

The design for the wrapper was simplified so that it could be printed on the linen case. This compromise made a poor wrapper and an even worse binding.

I was interested to find myself illustrating a Bible, and for children, so soon after the *Black Girl*. Although I had always wanted to illustrate the Bible, I felt Shaw's book would put an end to that ambition. Who would want an illustrator who had so 'impertinently smoked a cigarette over the body of Christ'? Yet such is the perversity of things, this was only the first of many biblical books I was to illustrate: perhaps I owed the others to De la Mare's book—it is difficult to say one way or the other.

BOOK-JACKET FOR 'THE POLITICAL MADHOUSE IN AMERICA AND NEARER HOME', BERNARD SHAW
(July 1933)
I engraved this in the Isle of Wight and took the block to the only printer on that isle, who said, 'I suppose this

is that new "Jill" Sans'. Maxwell said that he might just as well have set it in type and made a reverse block. It was a joke that had more than a grain of truth in it; but I prefer to think that the spacing and the design justified the engraving.

During August of this year I engraved five blocks for the *Strand Magazine*, illustrating a story by Michael Arlen. It appears I broke into the usual procedure by asking for galleys to make my own 'layout'—also by giving a star author lower-case initials. I am not sure whether there was a Special Board Meeting to sanction the latter, but it caused some consternation. Leech, the Art Editor, was an understanding man and gave me every help and encouragement, though he warned me of the peculiar problems of the magazine illustrator.

The unity so desirable in a book must be forgotten in the magazine. Every opening must be as different from the other as possible. The magazine is like a street of shops—each opening vying with the other to strike a new note.

I find nothing wrong with this restless vitality if one has that particular form of stamina. After all, what could be more attractive than the medley that is Piccadilly Circus? A different kind of unity is achieved; that is all. A cosmopolitan atmosphere is stimulating at times—my complaint is that only too often the magazines are not stimulating enough, but tend to wander along in a rather disconsolate and out-of-date manner. Bohemia is so often more respectable than the apparently respectable suburbs.

I would suggest that the English magazine brightens its pages a little if it is to compete in the market with its foreign relatives. For some reason the magazine market is world-wide; even the fashion magazine, that caterer for local contour, is becoming cosmopolitan.

I remember some interesting talks with Mrs. Settle when she was editing *Vogue*. She would inspire anybody who has the desire to become a fashion artist: she nearly converted me. I was experimental enough to play with the idea for a few days, but I explained to her that I could not change my job and alter my way of living. Fashion drawing is a full-time job, and I was already too interested in the variety of book work; besides, the speed of fashionable life did not appeal to me. It was a momentous decision, for I could have made much more money. I began to wonder, for the first time in my life, whether I was not a specialist after all. I am now convinced that, although there may be a certain amount of overlapping, there is a line somewhere drawn between the fashion artist, the publicity artist and the illustrator of books.

BOOK-JACKET FOR 'OVER THE RIVER', JOHN GALSWORTHY (August 1933)

This was another engraved lettering wrapper. The book appeared posthumously, and I was warned that Galsworthy's fastidious taste must be respected. We played for safety, cut out all pictorial motives, while decoration was reduced to a few wavy lines. The result was that I produced a wrapper that was criticized by the publishers as 'too quiet to stand out in the shop windows'; but a later report from them said that it showed well because it was such a quiet design! Sometimes one is lucky!

The advertisers must be constantly torn between the blatant bawling and the insidious whisper.

3rd June 1939

The first batch of boys of twenty years become conscripts to-day. I am reminded of the June of twenty-one years ago when I was called up at the age of eighteen. Such a vivid reminder gives an unpleasant hardness to the brilliantly sunny day, for I know that many of them must feel as I felt. How are they to know whether they will ever return to civilian life any more than I knew? I could only hope for a war to end. They can only hope that a war will not start.

True, it seems possible that we are in for a period of relaxation: September is the rumoured date for the next crisis.

I am glad I have no sons. It is bad enough to get fond of the boys one is teaching and to watch their difficulties. To see them being drawn into a grim machine is hard enough to bear. To have them return cynical would be still harder. It is to be hoped that they will make the personal effort of utilizing their experience and add to their stature as artists. My best hopes and wishes go with them.

This week-end nearly one hundred men were suffocated in the *Thetis*. We are so clever at making destructive machines that we must admire our skill and stifle our pity. The human race gets only what it deserves. We must harden up if we are to survive the conditions of to-day, and be ready to kill or be killed: the best way to prepare is to begin the killing, even if it is only in an amateur kind of way.

Those one hundred men know the best now—or the worst!

x

POSTER FOR 'ON THE ROCKS',
A PLAY BY BERNARD SHAW (November 1933)

London
16th November 1933

Dear John Farleigh,

Are you any good at posters? I badly need one for my new play, On the Rocks. *It is the ship of State that is on the rocks. A lovely medieval ship, the* Royal Harry, *poised on the top of a curly wave and about to come down crash on a rocky cliff with its high poop and balcony-like crow's nests and guns and royal standard all in the most beautiful order is what suggests itself.*

The thing they have printed—a huge . . . photograph of me—is so beastly that I must have something to outface it with. They think it lovely.

We produce on the 25th; so there is no time to be lost.

G. B. S.

Shaw 'phoned me to discuss it. I promised to let him have a rough by the evening, and arranged to take it to his Whitehall flat to be passed. When I arrived he looked at it for a while and then asked if he might show it to Mrs. Shaw, who was indisposed. He came back and said that they both felt the ship should have some figures showing (I had left them out), rather like 'the various statesmen watching, terrified, as the ship was about to be dashed on the rocks'. 'Otherwise it is excellent.'

I returned home, having arranged to meet Shaw the next morning at 10 o'clock at the Winter Garden Theatre (where he was rehearsing the play) with the finished poster for him to pass. I worked into the night

—finished the poster—not an ideal way of working—
and arrived at the box office, asked for the stage manager.
I explained that I was doing a poster for the play, and
was told very testily that there was no time for a poster
—it couldn't be done. I went to the stage door and
waited for Shaw. He arrived prompt to the minute,

walked me on to the middle of the stage, through the group of actors, who bade him good-morning, and there called for the production manager. He introduced me: 'This is John Farleigh, a very eminent artist. He is doing a poster for my play and I want you to give him every facility for finishing it.' I was taken back to the sultry box office—my instinct had been right not to argue but leave it to Shaw to handle—and given a dressing room to work in: some lettering, the phrasing of which I had been uncertain, was all that was left to be finished.

Finally I took it back to Shaw, and, when he had approved, I stood in the darkened auditorium and watched the rehearsal. Shaw sat in the centre of the stage facing his players and put them through their lines; occasionally he got up and showed them how it should be done.

It was a strange scene, and, as I left the theatre, I heard Shaw saying, 'No, no, no! This is how it should be done.' He looked very tall as he walked about the stage.

The poster was handed over and I was assured it would be safely handled.

London

28th November 1933

My dear Farleigh,

I am horrified: I thought I had sent the drawings back. I enclose three criticisms: the only ones I have to make. I am more pleased than ever, now that I have looked carefully through them.

The poster may not be posted; but it is all over the programs, which will be collected as art treasures.

When you have moved ask Miss Patch, my secretary, to

*get you tickets for the play. It isn't really ready yet, though
Saturday night was a huge success. The audience, however,
was picked and friendly.*

ever,

G. BERNARD SHAW

The drawings referred to were for the *Short Stories*.
I do not remember the reason for the hitch over the
poster—it was probably a question of time. I wish it had
never appeared, for I saw no proofs, as the job was
rushed, and when it did appear on the hoardings I
was aghast. Except for my signature it was not my
poster. I dashed off a letter to the theatre asking for an
explanation. The answer, after some delay, was an
unsatisfactory defence from the printer, and so I wrote
to Shaw. He answered:

London

6th January 1934

*I nearly died when I was told that 'the printer had got it
redrawn'. Macd. 'noticed that it did not look so well', but was
told that it would cost £50 to cancel and replace with a
photographed reproduction. I raged and refused to believe it;
and that is as far as we have got at present. But something
must be done, for I find the situation unbearable. Though I
haven't actually seen the damned thing the word 'redrawn'—
ugh! 'Runs not this speech like iron through your blood?'*

G. B. S.

The printers must have sent an explanation to Shaw
using various technical terms calculated to baffle anyone
but the expert, for he wrote me a letter:

London

14th January 1934

Dear John Farleigh,

The enclosed is all I can get out of the . . . people. We are children in these matters: the statement that '30″ × 40″ size is not used in the provinces' crushes me. We must master the etiquette of the hoardings.

I am more accustomed to these reverses than you are. When Ricketts's scenery for St. Joan was 'redrawn' for the provincial tour in order that his name and R.A. should be in the program our friendship received a blow from which it never recovered. He also was told that nobody would notice the difference. And nobody did. With great difficulty I persuaded him to let the R.A. stand . . . .

When the St. Pancras Vestry became a Borough Council and resolved to order a mace from Parkins and Gotto or somebody I induced them to have it designed for a prize by the students of the C. S. of Arts and Crafts. Carried unanimously. There was great excitement in the School. One day the Town Clerk took me into his office and displayed a Cromwellian mace, a triumph of the P. Gottesque. 'But what about the design?' I shrieked. 'There!' he said, pointing to an unfinished stalk on the thing (it was like a cauliflower being eaten by an octopus) leaving a cut-off end presenting a blank surface the size of a half crown: 'that is where the design is to go'.

I urged that the new seal should be designed by Walter Crane. The suggestion was ridiculed until the Mayor heroically declared that he agreed and would pay out of his own pocket Five Pounds to Mr. Crane for the design.

Somehow one survives these things. Nobody ever notices

the difference. Probably if they did they would all vote for the
trade article.

G. BERNARD SHAW

The explanation Shaw enclosed from the printer did
not baffle me, as I was used to their terms and their
excuses. I asked Shaw if I could approach the printers
personally and talk to them on equal terms. He replied:

All right: fight it out with them if you are happily young and
pugnacious enough to find it worth doing for the fun of it.
When people injure me I find it cheaper to pay them to go
away, even when crushing victory is within my reach.
  I'm writing to them to say that I leave them in your hands.

G. B. S.

16.1.34

The suggestion on the part of the printer that I did not
understand my job had got my back up, and so I called
on Macdona at the theatre full of fury, to say I would
fight the printer with his own jargon.

Macdona was very upset about the affair, and while
we were talking in the auditorium (I believe a play was
being rehearsed) who should be shown in but the very
printer himself, who was visiting London and had called
in on business.

Macdona begged me to let him down lightly as he
had, so far, done his work satisfactorily. But when we
were introduced he reiterated his criticism. He insisted
that the name of the theatre should have been on the
poster—forgetting that it was to be a double sheet—all
the information that he had crowded on to my design
was to have appeared on the sheet adjoining.

Self: 'Why did you not query this to me?'

Printer: 'There was not time to write.'

Self: 'What is wrong with the 'phone, and why did you redraw instead of making it a straightforward photo-litho job?'

Printer: 'We thought it would be too expensive and would look just as well redrawn and redesigned.'

Self: 'Then why put my name on it? Remember this, it is not your job to think about the redrawing or the expense. Query all doubts and then do your best to reproduce as well as possible in the way you are told to.'

Printer: 'I am sorry; the next edition of the poster I will have done properly.'

Self: 'It will be too late!'

The play came off too soon for the poster to be reprinted. My annoyance over the poster was mainly due to my keenness at that time to start making posters for the theatre. I still think it one of the best fields for the poster artist—the theatrical world does not seem to care how its plays are billed, for some obscure reason.

And so ended disastrously my only effort to prove that a good poster would advertise a play.

'SHORT STORIES, SCRAPS, AND SHAVINGS'
(1933)

The poster was made while this job was in progress, so I must revert to May, when I received a letter from William Maxwell. I had written to say how much I should miss his correspondence—in actual fact I find that Maxwell wrote to me several times a week, sometimes every day, while the *Black Girl* was in progress, and his letters were full of expert advice and friendliness—

I did not imagine there would be another Shaw book to illustrate for a long while, if ever.

Edinburgh
5th May 1933

Dear Farleigh,

Who said that we would lose touch with each other!

I saw G. B. S. last week, and he is now proposing to incorporate the Black Girl *in the* Short Story *volume of the Standard Edition, the publication of which has been held up until the time that the* Black Girl *in its present form should show signs of slacking off in sales. I at once saw the possibility of a difficulty in getting a good result on the Standard Edition paper, but somewhat to my surprise I found that we could get quite a tolerable result. I sent Shaw a sheet pulled on the Standard paper and he replies that the 'golden tone is a great improvement on the glare of the black-and-white, though that too has its special quality', and he adds, 'What does Farleigh think?'.*

So will you tell me what you think after seeing the sheet sent herewith, and will you address your reply to me at . . . W.1. I am going south to-night en famille *and will be there for the best part of a week. I shall be seeing Shaw some time during next week.*

I may tell you that Shaw also says, 'What I should really like if I could afford it is to get Farleigh to illustrate the whole volume'. Something might *come out of it.*

I knew that with my finicky additional alteration I should not get the wood-engraving of my bookplate before I left, but I wish I had had it, as it was my intention to have one of our girls along at the house during the week we are absent to stick in the bookplate and at the same time to give my books their annual dusting. I don't care, but my wife seems disappointed, as she thinks the dusting will need to proceed on its own and the bookplate operation be carried out later, but I have said No—a man must put his foot down sometimes!

Yours sincerely,

WILLIAM MAXWELL

Maxwell had commissioned me to engrave his bookplate—he was not exceptionally difficult to please, but a bookplate, like a portrait, is always a tricky job.

London

7th May 1933

Dear Farleigh,

Brandon Street has instructions to pull the bookplate on different papers in richest black and in darkish sepia and to leave one-sixteenth margin. I shall consult you before I print finally.

Shaw likes the golden tone and you indicate also approval. Your notes will be observed, but I ought to have told you that the make-ready was what was used on the Basingwerk and that a special make-ready will be used to adapt the work to the less suitable paper. I have told Shaw that while I had fears, experiment has proved them to be groundless and that I am now perfectly happy about the ultimate result.

A friend in N.Y. sent me an American B.G. and Shaw sent me one inscribed:

'To William Maxwell this American counterfeit of his work.　　　G. Bernard Shaw.'

I have suggested a middle course—why not have Farleigh do one full-page illustrating the 'high spot' in each story? I shall see him this week.　　　*Yours,*

W. M.

Proofs of the book were sent, and I made notes, suggestions, and a few sketches. Maxwell wrote me:

Ere now you have had the complete set of proofs of the Short Stories *and I shall be very interested to know what you have thought and what you have said to G. B. S. when you have come to a conclusion. Personally I hope the idea comes off.*

I wrote off my ideas to Shaw and enclosed a number of drawings, also giving an estimate of the cost of the illustrations as I had planned them. Shaw wrote:

Malvern

20th August 1933

Dear John Farleigh,

Forgive the delay: I have been working against time on the preparation of my new play for rehearsal, and have had to let everything else slide.

I am prepared to go as far as . . . . for the illustrations to the Short Stories; *so you may go ahead with your program. I enclose a hundred guineas for your immediate subsistence.*

In the picture of my knocking down the grandfather's clock the action is ambiguous and rather suggests my propping it up instead of pulling or shoving it down.

In the story called 'the Serenade' the instrument is a French horn, a quite peculiar and rather beautiful circular tube of brass, which the player holds with one hand in the bell (he can alter the notes in this way) and the other manipulating the pistons. The attitude is unlike that of the player of any other wind instrument, least of all a trumpet or trombone player. Before you draw it you must go to an orchestral concert (if there is one within reach) and study it from life. You cannot

mistake the horn player, because he is the only one who has his hand in the bell as he plays, and whose instrument is circular. The attitude is fatal to the notion of showing the notes as being blown out of the bell.

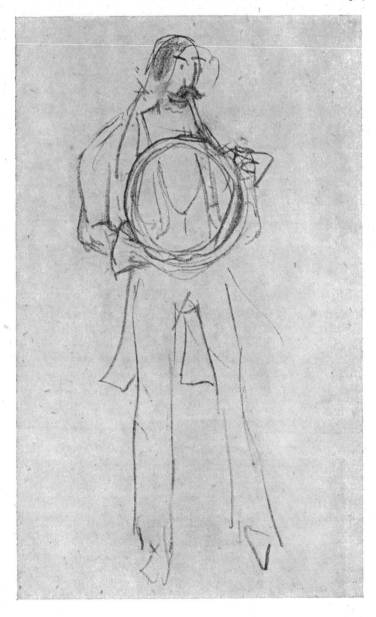

In 'Aerial Football' the last trumpet is a single slender straight tube, long enough to touch the ground in front of the trumpeter when pointed downward. This is too long for the modern Bach trumpet, but not for the Chinese bass trumpet, which is my notion of the apocalyptic one. Remember that the action of a trumpeter is not a puff but a dry spit: it draws in his cheeks instead of bulbing them out. You might puff through a trumpet for ten years without getting a sound from it. I know that this is contrary to the most cherished beliefs of all artists: but it is the cold fact.

I expect to be here until the middle of September or thereabouts.

always

G. BERNARD SHAW

On the drawing of the horn blower Shaw wrote, 'Horn blowers always look intensely melancholy.'

I opened the letter one morning while I was basking in the sun on the quietest coast I know—the south-west corner of the Isle of Wight. During this summer I worked from 6 a.m. until 9 a.m., and, after breakfast, kept the day free for painting or lazing. It was on this holiday that I first became interested in water-colours and produced sixty-five, of which number some half-dozen are still preserved as passable reminders of a delightful time.

I worked in a room in the farmhouse where I was staying and could watch the cows coming across the meadow in front of me for their first milking. These mornings were full of quiet pleasure in work and in anticipation of the day before me of swimming, painting and walking. I shared the skies with Turner and the farms with Morland, and to walk on the downs surrounded by the sea was to believe in Shakespeare.

Extract of letter from Maxwell, 31st August 1933.

You may be asked to do something for the title-page of the Omnibus Volume of Prefaces. *There is a big gap between title and imprint. I filled it with a rectangular block of type of the titles, but Shaw does not like it.*

I sent my completed drawings to Shaw in September; there was some delay, and I wrote to remind him.

London
9th November 1933

Dear John Farleigh,
    I am full of remorse for delaying you; but an adventure in which I got knocked down by a motor car, complicated by a journey to Edinburgh and daily rehearsals, prevented me from sitting down properly to the pictures. But you may go ahead with them: they are first rate; only don't engrave the sneezing bust of Shakespeare yet: I may have a suggestion to make about it.
    In haste—chronic for the moment—
                G. BERNARD SHAW

A short while after three drawings came from him—the suggestion for Shakespeare and two others.

The blocks were engraved in the gradual course of time, everything was passed; it seemed merely a matter of finishing.

*Drawing by Bernard Shaw for 'Short Stories, Scraps,
and Shavings'*

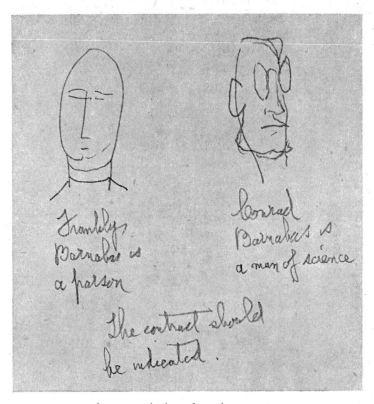

Drawing by Bernard Shaw for 'Short Stories, Scraps, and Shavings'

Y

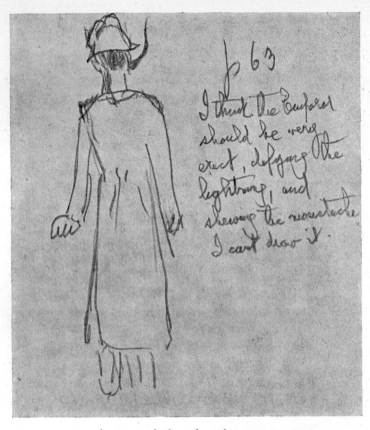

Drawing by Bernard Shaw for 'Short Stories, Scraps,
and Shavings'

Extract from letter to Maxwell from Shaw dated 18th November 1933:

Farleigh has done a superb poster for On the Rocks. *I am greatly tempted to get him to do an Elizabethan title-page for the* Prefaces.

This comment was made before Shaw saw the proofs of the poster.

'SHORT STORIES' PREFACE

London

6th December 1933

Dear John Farleigh,

Maxwell is producing an omnibus volume of my Prefaces; *and the enclosed is the title-page. It revolts me. Why not a picture title-page? Have you ever studied the old ones? The ones that consisted of a grand display of every fount in the printer's stock are no use in this case, because there is no letterpress except* PREFACES BERNARD SHAW CON- STABLE & CO 1933; *so the pictorial, monumental masonic, cornucopian style with muses and torches and emblems round a fearfully impressive portrait is what occurred to me. But that was only for a start: what it will filter down to, or expand to in your imagination and skilled hands, Heaven only knows. Let it incubate, and then tell me whether you feel disposed to take it on.*

always,

G. B. S.

The two drawings by Shaw that accompanied this letter are shown in the following pages.

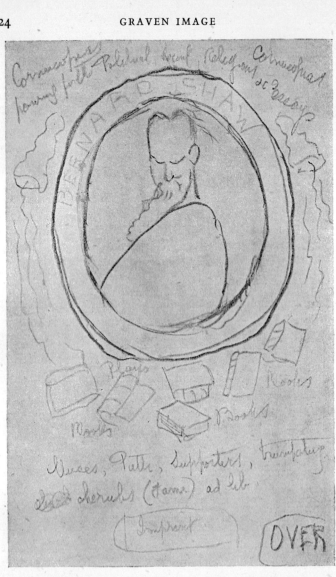

Drawing by Bernard Shaw for 'Prefaces' Title-page

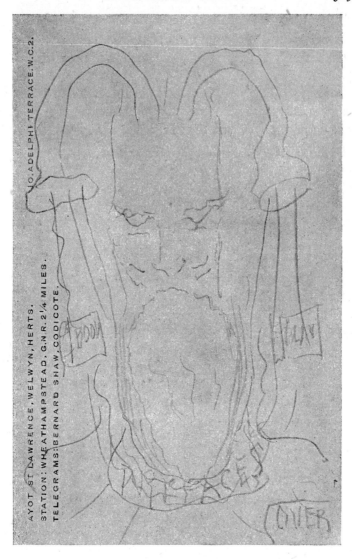

Drawing by Bernard Shaw for 'Prefaces' Title-page

I sent off a reproduction of a seventeenth-century pictorial title-page, saying that I would like to do something as full of incident. It came back with the comment:

The only objection to it is that as a whole *it's damned ugly; but I daresay you can get over that. It looks more like a picture page than a frontispiece. However, let yourself rip; and fix your own price: damn the expense!*

G. B. S.

30.12.33

On 9th January, Maxwell wrote:

London

Dear Farleigh,

Can you tell me what you are doing for the Short Stories *? Are all your cuts full pages or are they varied in size?*

I want to get at the total extent of the volume so as to fix paper quantity and bulk. I know what the book makes, but what are you adding to it in extent?

Yours ever,

WILLIAM MAXWELL

I sent off the necessary information.

Edinburgh

Dear Farleigh,

I have had some discussion with G. B. S. regarding the headlines to the stories in the Short Story *volume. To have retained them as in the proof you have would have involved adding headlines to the* Black Girl *story, but I have got him entirely off the headlines and they will all be removed, retaining only the title headings to the individual stories.*

Then he says, 'Has Farleigh sent you the blocks yet?'

And again, 'Is it possible to mend a block as you mend an electro of type? In the Black Girl, *p. 59, he has spelt Genesis Genises; and people write blaming poor me for this illiteracy.' As he has raised the question I think I had better send you the block to have it plugged with the correct spelling of Genesis, and we shall make a new electro of it for insertion at p. 59 of the* Black Girl.

Don't get excited about his request as to whether you have sent the blocks yet, but give me some idea as to when we are to have them. The present proposal is that the book shall be published at Easter.

As I am writing may I repeat my expression of the hope that your engraving throughout will be such as to make it not too difficult to print the illustrations on the paper of the Standard Edition. It will be somewhat of a task to get as good an effect on this considerably rougher surfaced paper with its yellow tone as we can on the Basingwerk parchment used for the Black Girl.

I am going south to-night, will be in London Tuesday– Wednesday only, and it is my intention, if possible, to drop in and see you at the Central School, but I cannot say at what hour. If you send me a note to the Club to-morrow saying if you are available between 4 and 6 on Wednesday, that would suit me nicely.

Yours sincerely,

WILLIAM MAXWELL

My paste-up of twelve blocks went off to Edinburgh, and I received a letter from Maxwell's secretary to tell me of their safe arrival.

Edinburgh

17th January 1934

Dear Sir,

We have received the 12 blocks mentioned in your letter of 15th January and also the drawings showing positions. When we send you proofs of the pages we shall also let you have these drawings back in order that you may check our placing. We note that the last of the blocks will be in our hands a fortnight from now.

Yours faithfully,

R. & R. CLARK, LIMITED

(Sgd.) BLAIR MAXWELL,

Secretary

On the same date a note came from Maxwell, who was in London, enlarging the point of a telephone conversation he had had with my wife on the 16th.

London

17th January 1934

Title-page for Prefaces

All I am concerned about is that the paper is thin, and while sufficiently opaque for the type it might not be for your engraving if there are any solids. Even an odd bit of solid here and there would shine through as spots on the verso. I gather from Elsie that the answer is 'fear nothing', so I shall fix up the paper to-morrow.

Have you by chance thought of a title opening, the title occupying the two pages left and right? It is probably not quite expedient in a vol. which, though not so called, is somewhat of an omnibus.

When am I to get your title-page? No hurry, *but I'd like to have an idea.*

W. M.

Edinburgh

20th January 1934

Dear Farleigh,

Many thanks for your letter. I think you are under a misapprehension that what I was asking about was the title-page for the Short Story *volume. I am not concerned about it as there is no question of handling it on a thin paper. It will be on 120 lb. paper, which will present no difficulty as to opacity. What I spoke to Elsie about on the phone was the title-page for the Omnibus volume of* Prefaces. *It is on a thin paper, and what I was anxious about was that it should not contain anything so heavy that it would unduly shine through a paper which of necessity cannot be completely opaque. It will be opaque enough for the type, but if there was anything in the nature of a solid or bits of solid I am quite sure the effect on the verso would be bad.*

I gathered from Elsie that your idea in connection with it was towards something that would give a general grey effect. If that is so I am not worried, but if you look at the Omnibus Plays *and see how even there the type shows through on the back of the title-page, you will see exactly what I want to avoid. The Omnibus* Prefaces *paper will, however, be 25% thicker than the paper of the Omnibus* Plays *and that will go so far as to correct the danger which I feared. I am also having it made of a furnish which will be slightly more opacity-producing.*

I am interested in all you say about your new technique. It will be all to the good as there will be very few books you will

*have the chance of doing in which you have the benefit of such
a paper as Basingwerk Parchment as used for the Black Girl.*

   *Will hope to see you at the Double Crown Club Dinner.
I am rather in hopes that your title-page for the Prefaces will
come in not any longer than four weeks hence—perhaps
earlier.*

Yours sincerely,

WILLIAM MAXWELL

The new technique referred to was a movement to
get away from the solid blacks and complicated textures
and design in black lines and a single grey tone.

A few of the blocks in the *Short Stories* show this
tendency, and I thought it a good idea to exploit the idea
on the *Prefaces* title-page, since Maxwell wanted a light
block for the thin paper.

Edinburgh

22nd January 1934

Dear Farleigh,

   *I have a card from Mr. Shaw's secretary to say that Mr. and
Mrs. Shaw are leaving for New Zealand on February 8.
That's O.K. with me as America says, but will your work be
so far advanced that we are at liberty to print the Short Story
volume with all your illustrations, or will he have seen proofs
of your engravings, or does he not see them, i.e. having passed
the drawings you go ahead without further reference to him?
Another point—shall we have had all your engravings in
time to let us get the book re-made up with the woodcuts
inserted so that he may have a final glance through the proof?
As to the Omnibus volume, the Preliminary of this is not yet
arranged, as it depends upon your title-page. Will he have*

*seen enough of your title-page design to authorise us to go
ahead with the printing?*

*The intention as to the Omnibus Prefaces is that it shall be
published about one month after the three plays volume now
printing, and I fancy it will be published in three weeks, or
perhaps four from now.*

*I don't know if I made clear in my last that I understand
from what you said about the Short Stories volume that you
are giving us an engraved title-page for it, but that is what I
took from what you said.*

*I shall not be in London this week, but will be on Tuesday
and Wednesday next week.*

Yours sincerely,

WILLIAM MAXWELL

Shaw passed all the blocks except for one, which he
returned with a drawing in ink pasted over the bishop;
underneath was the comment:

*This is my only criticism—too late to bother about. The reason
the bishop arrived after the woman was that in an excess of
bumptious energy he insisted on cutting off the corners instead
of sticking to the path.*

I plugged the block and engraved the bishop according to this suggestion.

Edinburgh

26th January 1934

Dear Farleigh

*Since I wrote you I have heard from Kyllmann that he
suggested to Shaw (and in a letter from Shaw this morning
there is no reference, so he apparently has no objection) that*

the Omnibus Preface *volume be delayed until publication in July. If that is really the case then you need not hurry, but I am not quite clear about one remark by Shaw which may possibly apply to the Omnibus. He says, 'I hope Farleigh will be able to let me see the frontispiece—or title-page—before I go; but if not you and he must go ahead without me. The same applies to the arrangement of the blocks in* Short Stories.' *I fancy that this applies to* Short Stories *and that what he has in mind is an engraved title-page. The* Black Girl *comes at the end of the volume, so there would be no objection to having an engraved title-page to open the volume with. In fact I think it is essential, as it would look rather weak to have an ordinary type title-page opening the volume and then giving the very last story a fully engraved title-page of its own.*

My idea of a double title-page for the Prefaces *volume— but I have no authority to ask you to do it and it would need to come as a suggestion from you—is to have your fully engraved title-page on the left and a page facing it which would serve as Contents surrounded by an engraved border to harmonise and balance with the title-page. It might be that this Contents would be rather difficult to treat typographically, and that the type would need to be pretty small, but you can think it out. I enclose proof of the actual matter that will appear in the Contents. I don't think your suggestion of having all the plays filling out the whole page is a sound one. It would be all right if all the prefaces belonged to plays, but there are prefaces which stand entirely by themselves and which have no connection with any of the plays, e.g.* Killing for Sport, *the* Prison Reform *preface and others. You will see them for yourself in the enclosed proof.*

Short Stories *again. When we get the remainder of the blocks the* Short Stories *volume will be at once made up*

according to your layout, and you will get a set of proofs.
I fancy there will be nothing to discuss. The only thing you
have to think about is the title-page.

Yours sincerely,

WILLIAM MAXWELL

The drawing for the *Prefaces* title-page was made and
sent off to Shaw.

Welwyn

5th February 1934

I sail on Thursday for N.Z. and shall not be back until May.
I am so distracted with packing and other preparations that I
haven't the least notion of whether I have left anything
unsettled with you. Will you let me have a line by return to
4 Whitehall Court to enlighten me?

I have the Prefaces title-page and will return it to-morrow,
but have I paid for it?

G. BERNARD SHAW

The drawing came back on the 7th February signed
'O.K. G. B. S. 7.2.34'. I wrote asking Shaw for a
photograph to use in the title-page, and Shaw wrote:

London

8th February 1934

Dear John Farleigh,

If you arrange with my secretary, Miss Patch, beforehand
you can come in at any time and look through the cabinet of
photographs of me which are shoved in there as they come, and
left until somebody begs for one and selects it.

I got the set of proofs safely. Many thanks.

I wish some revolutionary ultra-modern would persuade the printers to use black ink. It seems to me to get slatier and slatier on the way to becoming invisible ink.

Just off to New Zealand. Back in May.

always,

G. B. S.

The next day he 'phoned me about some last-minute arrangements, and said he wanted an engraved title-page for the *Short Stories*. I mentioned that he would be unable to see the design before it appeared in the book, to which he replied that he would leave it entirely in my hands.

Edinburgh

Dear Farleigh,

Your proposition that we should eliminate the half-titles and blanks would entirely upset the Short Story volume. On the present arrangement it will be 316 pp. If each story just commences a right- or left-hand page as it happened to fall and with the half-titles taken away the extent would be 280 pp. It really would not do to reduce the thickness of the volume by so much as 36 pp.

I enclose a copy of the Contents with the dates attached where we know them. There are two stories, 'Beauty's Duty' and 'The Domesticity of Franklyn Barnabas', for which we do not have a date. Ring up Miss Patch and see if she can give them.

G. B. S. has laid down the law as to the construction of the title, and instead of my arrangement, which I thought it wise to submit to begin with, he wants you brought right into the title along with himself, so that, as he himself expresses it, you may have every chance of good press notices and reviews. You will see the new title in due course.

I have word from Kyllmann confirming that the Black Girl *engraved title-page is not to appear in the* Standard *volume. I am quite pleased. He also tells me that we may have an engraved title-page—that, of course, has been superseded by your suggestion for an engraving facing the title—and that he has arranged with you that he is to see the design, and adds, 'If we finally approve it we will ask him to engrave it'. He also tells me that the design for the title-page of the* Prefaces *has been finally approved.*

I am sorry that I not only omitted to write you when I got the set of proofs of the Short Stories *engravings, but I also forgot to mention them when I saw you the day before yesterday. Thank you very much indeed for letting me have these.*

Yours sincerely,

WILLIAM MAXWELL

The title-page for *Short Stories* was drawn from a model of some shavings placed in a dramatic light. The pattern of the curled shavings and cast shadows made a design that I thought sufficient in itself apart from adding the various dates to show when the stories were written. The edges of the block were left roughly finished, while in the bottom corner was engraved the point of my graver in the act of clearing the wood. Scraps and shavings seemed to be the motive to illustrate; the short stories would look after themselves, apart from the dates, which were engraved on the shavings, rather as legends were written on the scrolls of the stained-glass window.

Edinburgh
19th February 1934

Dear Farleigh,

Thanks for the remainder of the proofs of the Short Stories *volume. The only thing we now require is the engraved frontispiece to face the title-page. It will be all right if it is here on Monday the 26th. As already mentioned, we shall keep the page slightly lower so that no one of the headings will be without a small margin of paper above it in the trimmed volume. You won't see any further proofs as we are making electroplates of the book, including the illustrations as the drawings come back from you, and the next stage will be printing, but you may leave it to us quite safely.*

I shall be very interested to see even your drawing of the title-page for the Prefaces *if you can spare it when the time comes. If not, I must wait until I see a proof of the engraved block.*

I am very sorry indeed to hear that you have been suffering the afflictions of Job, but I don't believe it. I think the real facts are that you are afflicted to an extent which in comparison with your capacity for patience is perhaps greater than Job's! I hope you got on all right at Cambridge on Saturday, and that all the troubles that afflicted the just and the unjust will have disappeared before you get this letter.

Yours sincerely,

WILLIAM MAXWELL

Edinburgh
23rd February 1934

Dear Farleigh,

Constable's are urging us to give an early date for completion of the printing of Short Stories. *We want two things from you, the most urgent being the engraving which you had back for alteration—I wired you about it—and the other is the frontispiece, which I am expecting from you at the moment, the sooner the better.*

Yours sincerely,

WILLIAM MAXWELL

Edinburgh
9th March 1934

Dear Farleigh,

Very many thanks for the proofs.

The Story Volume is printed and will go to binders next week. I understand Constable will publish somewhere 'about Easter'. but I have no knowledge of actual date.

Will be in London on Monday just for the day.

Yours,

W. M.

The *Prefaces* title-page had now to be drawn. I obtained permission (and photographs) from Sybil Thorndike and Cedric Hardwicke, showing them in the parts of Joan, in *St. Joan*, and the King, in *The Apple Cart*. They appeared in the niches at each side of Shaw's head, which was distorted to give the sense of elongation; cornucopias grew from his head like long horns and swung downwards, pouring out MSS. of the plays, while the Black Girl springs from his head like Minerva, fully armed. Mr. and Mrs. Everyman sit in perilous positions on the upper cornice; scenes from *Androcles* and *Man and Superman* appear on the lower panels; while the imprint is supported by the printer, shown in a bowler

z

hat, and the publisher, shown in a top hat. The shyness of the publisher is indicated by his turning away from the audience. These figures are not portraits.

I amused myself very much over this design; it is not often one gets the chance of making a title-page for an 'omnibus' of such importance.

> *Edinburgh*
> *14th May 1934*

Dear Sir,

We acknowledge block for the title-page of the Shaw Prefaces *volume safely to hand to-day.*

> *Yours faithfully,*
> R. & R. CLARK, LIMITED
> (*Sgd.*) BLAIR MAXWELL,
> *Secretary*

The *Short Story* volume came out quietly just as the whole procedure had been quiet. I believe that few people know of it, compared with those who know the *Black Girl*, though it contains better engravings than in that first book I made for Shaw.

There is no doubt that the prettiness of the Black Girl was responsible for her popularity, yet this was a quality I was completely unconscious of at the time. I knew that I liked her, but was not aware that she would have a popular appeal.

I have told the story of the *Short Stories* almost entirely through the letters of Shaw and the printer. These letters are eloquent enough of the job, and prove, beyond all question, that Maxwell's part in the making of the book was as important as mine. And yet, wise as he is in the ways of printing, he is always prepared to act on a suggestion from the artist who is working for him: even to the extent of making that artist feel that he, Maxwell, is working under his directions. His letters show his ability to guide and advise in a friendly and tactful manner.

Every illustrator would be advised to make close contact with his printer: he will learn one aspect of his job from this source that can be learned nowhere else.

Shaw sent me a copy of the *Short Stories* inscribed:

To John Farleigh, who has done most of the shaving,
                    G. Bernard Shaw, 25th May 1934

Later in the year I discovered I had not sent in my bill for the *Short Stories* title-page, and Shaw answered:

                                        Malvern
                            15th September 1934
Dear John Farleigh,
   I enclose cheque with apologies.
   It is a great relief to me to know that you not only keep accounts but occasionally refer to them.
   Heaven help you if you rely on my bookkeeping!
                        ever,
                        G. BERNARD SHAW

The next few pages are concerned with progressive proofs of the *Short Stories* and *Prefaces* engravings. They may be useful to some student of engraving.

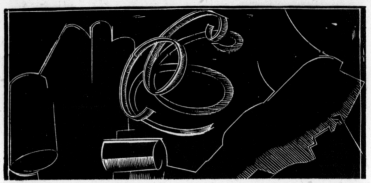

1st state

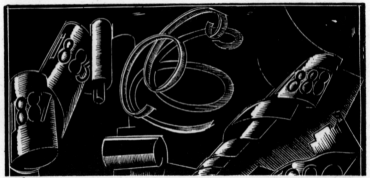

2nd state

3rd state   *Progressive proofs of title-page for 'Scraps*
                    and Shavings', by Bernard Shaw

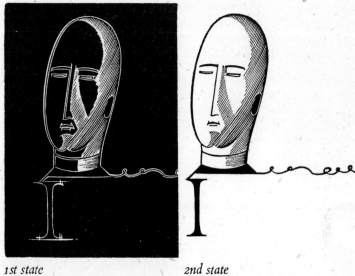

1st state   2nd state

1st state   2nd state

Progressive proofs of two headings for ' Scraps and Shavings ',
by Bernard Shaw

1st state

2nd state

3rd state

Progressive proofs of illustration for 'Scraps and Shavings',
by Bernard Shaw

Progressive proofs of title-page for 'Prefaces by Bernard Shaw'

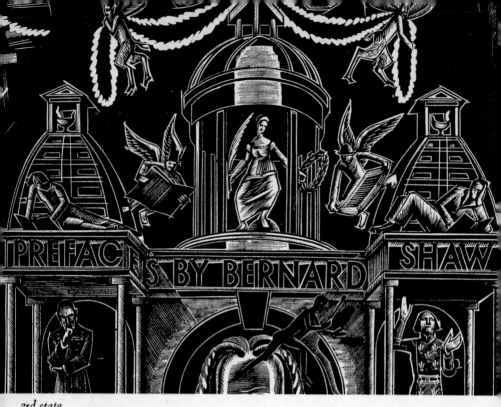

3rd state

Progressive proofs of title-page for 'Prefaces by Bernard Shaw'

4th state

'THE WAY OF ALL FLESH' (1934)

The publishers suggested that if Shaw would write a Preface it would make an interesting addition to this book, which was to celebrate its emergence from the laws of copyright. I wrote to suggest this to Shaw, although I felt it was asking more than could be expected; the answer did not disappoint me:

Welwyn

29th May 1934

Dear John Farleigh,

Many thanks for the proofs, which are waiting for me in London.

Butler is impossible, for the reason given on the enclosed stock p.c. Besides, my old boost of Butler, which put him regularly on the map, has been so much quoted during the last ten years or so that there would be nothing fresh about it. It would add nothing perceptible to combined weight of Butler and Farleigh.

I was amazed and delighted by the cure for the bishop.

G. B. S.

The last phrase refers to the block for the *Short Stories*, which had been altered while Shaw was away.

Butler's was the first novel I had had to illustrate, and the first reading made me realize that a careful analysis of the story was necessary before I could begin to make any drawings at all.

I learnt, in this job, a method that can be applied to all novels.

1. *A rapid reading of the whole book.* Any suggestion of a possible illustration is marked in the margin. This

first impact is important—it is the most personal moment of the artist; when his imagination alone is colouring the narrative. The fact that fifty possible designs are marked is no matter, for the list can be reduced easily enough at the next stage when the scheme for the illustrations is being more carefully planned.

2. *Selection of illustrations from first list.* The final number must depend on fees and the artist's market value. The designs must be spread through the book to appear at approximately regular intervals. Again, careful selection must give prominence to designs in the sections of the book that are prominent in themselves; the smaller designs should lead up to the important ones. Thus, waves of illustrations will correspond to the ebb and flow of the story. A careful word picture should be made of each illustration, with a rapid sketch of the complete set of drawings, each one in relation to its final status on the printed page.

It is advisable to leave the job for a few days, or even weeks. The images sink back into the subconscious and develop of their own accord. It is the usual process of gestation known to every artist.

3. *Second reading of the book.* This is done slowly and with care, for it is a search for any detail that will throw light on the incidents and characters to be illustrated. A chart is made of these details that will save the designer any further trouble of re-reading. The necessary information can then be seen at a glance.

Every characteristic, every habit and scrap of description that seems of importance to the true delineation of characters must be written down. In this way the

	Hero's Mother	Hero's Uncle	Hero's Aunt	Hero	Hero's Wife
	Pale oval face, blue eyes, restless mouth, long hands, usually in black.			Born.	
	Died	Fat, short, fair hair, short beard, fidgets with watch chain.	Thin, hard features, small mouth, high lace collar, hands nearly always folded.	Like Mother, pale face, tall, thin, lace collar, looks restless.	
		Thinner, bald—a little short-sighted.	Died.	Married, rather tall, elegant movement, fashionable clothes, good hands, nervous movements.	Tallish, well built, easy movements, round face, dark hair, good taste.
		Invalid in chair—talkative, in irritating manner		Slight stoop, looks much older—dress rather careless.	Died.
		Died		Definite stoop, brooding air, uses hands to express himself a lot, clothes good, but rather shabby.	

illustrator will get to know the characters as well as the author must have done. If the page number is included with every entry a later reference to the book will be made easy.

The illustrator should be able to work from this chart without reference to the book except for an occasional re-reading of a passage or chapter where designs may need revision.

Information of backgrounds should be gathered in the course of this second reading. It is important to note that a full description of the background does not always appear around the incident, but may have to be gathered from the rest of the book.

This process of collecting detail is somewhat akin to detective work, and while the evidence is being collected the imagination will be playing with all the possible factors and evolving a solution as fresh evidence comes to light. I have no theory that imagination can do without, or be impeded by detail, and, since illustrations need detail, it may as well be pertinent detail.

4. *The final drawings are made*. The first rough sketches should be scrutinized carefully, for they contain much of the final design in them, and, what is more important, they have the original contact of the artist's mind with the book before it has become complicated with accumulated detail. Many a finished drawing has lost all originality and vigour owing to the first rough sketch being ignored. With the help of the chart this sketch can be developed into the final drawing.

From now on the job of the illustrator is to bring his drawing to life. All parts, characters, and objects must

be arranged and knit together to create an atmosphere
that is consistent with the imagination of the artist—no
amount of detail on the part of the author need prevent
an artist from making his own interpretation, and at the
same time satisfy his author. The National Gallery is full
of pictures by artists who had just as many restrictions
placed upon them—which makes it unnecessary to add
any remarks about details restricting the creative powers
of the artist.

Collecting books of reference for this job filled my
shelves with periodicals and bound volumes, and my
interest in nineteenth-century illustration began with
the acquisition of these books. This is part of the pleasure
of breaking new ground.

The search among the markets of London for old
books that may be useful is not commercially sound, but
I consider the loss of a few hours of money-earning well
worth while if it is spent browsing among dusty books.

I look back at the book and think it is good in parts.
At the time I wished it could have been as profusely
illustrated as in Cruikshank's day.

When the book appeared I sent a copy to Shaw, who
wrote:

London

15th January 1935

Dear John Farleigh,

Many thanks for The Way of All Flesh. *But what a
dangerous job! If I had to reflect on and visualize that book
for a month I should be permanently injured—worse than if
I had spent a year in hell.*

I knew Butler. The illustrations are diabolically good.

I am not sure about the lecture on the 25th January. I have had to put off my voyage to South America, my wife being ill and my domestic affairs in confusion. But I will come if I can.

faithfully,

G. BERNARD SHAW

Shaw came to my lecture on Book Illustration, which was given to the Society of Scribes at Queen's Square. I showed some of his drawings for the *Black Girl* on the screen, and he enjoyed them as much as the audience did. The discussion afterwards was started, and kept going, by him.

I was very gratified that he should have come at all, and more so that he should show such an active interest in the discussion. It was very kind of him. I went with him to the door afterwards. His car was not there and, as it was a cold showery evening, I asked if I could call him a taxi. He refused the idea and said he was going to walk home and get some fresh air. He went off with more of my affection and admiration than ever.

1st state

2nd state

Progressive proofs for 'Way of All Flesh', by Samuel Butler

1st state

2nd state

Progressive proofs for 'Way of All Flesh', by Samuel Butler

3rd state   *4th state*

Progressive proofs for 'Way of All Flesh', by Samuel Butler

2 A

'THE STORY OF DAVID', A. &. C. BLACK
(June 1934)

This was intended, if successful, to be the first of a series of illustrated Bible stories printed direct from the Bible in prose form. *The Story of David* was collected from different parts of the Bible and included some of the Psalms. It made a good thriller with David as an early example of a gangster who put a husband on the spot.

In general make-up I followed the *Black Girl* very closely—in fact, it resembles that job in many of its details. The blocks were finished and the book made up from the galleys before the publishers saw so much as a sketch. When I presented the paste-up there was general consternation. Not only was the book not in the tradition of A. & C. Black's, but my designs were considered doubtful matter for reproduction owing to a few nudes; that of David in particular, who 'danced naked before the Lord'. For a short period it was considered advisable to sell the book and me to a publisher who was more likely to favour the work. Maxwell, who was printing the book, was asked his advice. His reply was not revealed to me by the publisher, but the book went ahead, so I gathered *he* had no scruples about my naked figures, and a very beautiful printing job he made of it.

I looked forward to making some more books in this series, but the travellers were not used to such productions; they could not sell *David*. A friend who tried to buy one was advised to go to the R.S.P.C.K.—it was only too probable that this Society had refused to buy the book. All this shows how much a book depends on the travellers. *The Story of David* is now submerged with

all the other remainders—where do all the remainders
go, I wonder!

*Details of blocks for
'The Story of David'*

'CAPE FAREWELL', CRESSET PRESS

This was the first book that I illustrated with pen drawings, and they show a mixture of styles, since I was amusing myself with methods of using the pen. They share, in common with all the pen drawings I have made since, a distinct tendency towards decorative fantasy.

I don't think I am bored with the graphic drawing, yet I can never keep myself to a simple, objective statement. Yes! I *am* bored with the purely graphic. Every drawing, print, painting or piece of stone must have some significance beyond its technical accomplishment and its objective value. There is a certain irrational quality about real life that must not be lost. The critic who looks at a painting and says he does not quite understand a certain passage had best look to himself. Those who desire to understand in order to appreciate had best beware, lest they begin to question their own irrelevancies.

'THREE FANTASTIC TALES',
BY CLAUDE HOUGHTON

If ever a writer gives reign to the fantastic it is Claude Houghton. I have read all his books with the greatest of pleasure and always with the desire to illustrate him one day. This book had only one pen drawing—a frontispiece—and as the drawing progressed I became almost frightened of it myself. I used to go into my studio and look at it, wondering whether it had changed of its own accord, or whether I should destroy it before the figures moved. Houghton sent me a copy inscribed:

for John Farleigh, in admiration, Claude Houghton.

It is strange that so few mystery books are illustrated. Perhaps publishers, or the public, fear that illustrations will dispel the mystery.

It shows a poor knowledge of the power of drawing if this is the reason.

SERIAL STORY FOR A NEWSPAPER

Phone message:

Newspaper: 'Can you illustrate a story about Malays—or do you only draw African natives?'

Self: 'I see no reason why not, I have only drawn one black girl.'

An interview later because the drawings are not quite satisfactory.

The Editor: 'These drawings are not what we expected.'

Self: 'What did you expect?'

The Editor: 'Something like the Black Girl.'

Self: 'They were wood-engravings; these are pen drawings.'

The Editor: 'Also we do not like the girl, she is not pretty enough.'

Self: 'If you study some photographs of these people you will see that I have done the best I can with them—they are not pretty.'

The Editor: 'Her arms are out of drawing.'

Self: 'What do you mean by that?'

The Editor: 'They are too long.'

Self: 'That is a characteristic of these natives.'

The Editor: 'Another of our editors has been to Malay

and seen these people. He says their hair is not fuzzy as you have drawn it.'

Self to other Editor: 'Were you long in Malay?'

Other Editor: 'I landed for a few days.'

Self: 'You realize that Malay is an archipelago and has many tribes, and that this is one of them.'

To Editor: 'What you really mean is that these drawings are not what you want.'

The Editor: 'Quite! I will show you the sort of drawings we like at the moment.' Turns over files and shows me drawings by other artists.

Self: 'But if that is the sort of drawing you want, why didn't you get that artist to do them? I do not work that way. If I thought my drawings were bad I would redraw them, but you have not convinced me.'

The Editor: 'Our artists get used to our requirements after a while and produce the sort of drawings we like.'

Self: 'Then you must go to them and not to me. I will not imitate a style if I have no desire to do so. Incidentally another paper has seen these drawings and admired them.'

The Editor: 'Which paper is that?'

Self: 'I am sorry but I cannot tell you.'

The drawings appeared, though they were heralded by an apology—'Illustrated by unusual drawings by John Farleigh', and I heard nothing from that newspaper to this day. It was worth the battle—even if I did lose it. At least, I am not groaning while I do pretty girls and slick drawings.

In the autumn I engraved a large block of the Creation of Eve. It is almost entirely solid black and represents the extreme point of fine white lines and stipple. It seems a reversion from the *Prefaces* title-page technique that I was so excited about early in the year. I think I wanted to shroud the subject in the mystery of dark tones, and probably overdid it.

The Exhibition of British Industrial Art at the Royal Academy brought me two experimental jobs from Poole Potteries and Oliver Hill.

For Poole Potteries I designed a large panel of Adam and Eve that was made in coloured tiles. Some of them were modelled slightly. It was rather similar to designing a stained-glass window. My studio was too low for the drawing, which was fifteen feet high, so the paper travelled across the ceiling as I worked. I made the working drawing just as a stained-glass artist makes his key drawing, and numbered the spaces from specimen tiles that had been sent to me. A shaded edge showed where low relief was needed, and I left the rest to the Potteries. I tried out a full-colour sketch in the Academy, which was as yet quite empty, and the final result was surprisingly satisfactory.

Oliver Hill asked me to decorate the walls of an out-door dining room, one wall of which was open to the garden. The other three, made of marble, were to be decorated with sandblast designs. He explained the process and asked for a sketch design on the spot as there were only a few days left. I sketched out a rough, and, with his plans, returned to make my designs in separate panels and send them off as I completed them, so that the sandblasting could go ahead without delay.

It was finished in time: both jobs provided me with some interesting experience in decorative work.

'THE MAN WHO DIED' (1935)

As I read this book I visualized it as illustrations: I was so keen to do it that I approached the publishers and explained my ideas. Frere Reeves, of Heinemann, was equally enthusiastic about the book, agreed to publish, and left the design of the whole thing in my hands, providing I kept within costs.

I rushed off to Mason, full of excitement, and we discussed ideas together. He brooded for weeks over the title-page, with the result that we had one of the loveliest title-pages I have ever seen in a book. I showed him my designs as we went along, and it was his suggestion that we should use red. He seemed to be as responsible for the designs as I was. When I look back on our discussions it seems that we must have worked very close together: I do not remember clearly who was responsible for any particular part of the book, Mason or myself.

The use of one colour and black is full of possibilities, and red in this particular book was all I needed to give full reign to the subcurrent of intensity that Lawrence had got into the story. I made the red ebb and flow as the story sank into passivity or increased in intensity.

Mason's title-page struck a rich note with its red and black. His subtle play on the words and use of Roman and Gothic give it a ceremonial and chant-like quality. This was his intention, and he derived his inspiration from the early psalters. That seems to me to be the true value of tradition. His design is as modern as can be, and yet it derives from early traditional motives. He set the type solid and removed all quotation marks. 'This', he said, 'won't make it easy to read, but it's a book that should be read slowly—almost in a chant—anyway, neither your work nor mine is for lazy people.'

Mason is a true artist: he does not compromise when he is working on a good job; and he made a good job of this. I learned as much about type design from him as I shall ever learn, and I am grateful to him.

The drawings were made as simple wash drawings; I was experimenting in drawing with broad sweeps of the brush, and this shows in the simple blacks and grey tones of the engravings. Texture was almost eliminated. Mason wanted light blocks with plenty of white and grey and the minimum of black.

I enjoyed doing this book, and I still feel it to be one of the best I have made. This Mason is responsible for; his setting is superb; it would be difficult not to work well with him.

It is now remaindered. Lawrence's reputation suffered a reverse just before we published, and the book never sold well. Perhaps, also, it is not a book that would ever be popular. Lewis, of the Cambridge University Press, printed it as well as any book could be printed. I lost money over this job, just as the publishers must have done. Frere Reeves was charming enough to say that he would be prepared to lose more money on another book as beautiful. When I can afford to lose money on a book again I shall remind him of his statement. I know that he will be as willing as he professed to be.

Lady Ottoline Morrell wrote me:

21st December

Dear Mr. Farleigh,

How good of you to send me that beautiful book. I am delighted to have it and admire your illustrations very much.

They are, I feel, what D. H. Lawrence himself would have liked—it is a very beautiful book and it makes me sad that it was the last work of Lawrence—I wish he could have lived.

Yours sincerely,

OTTOLINE MORRELL

The progressives are shown with proofs of the red blocks printed in black separately. Register ticks can be seen in the red blocks. These ticks had to be covered by the black for the red block to be traced.

Progressive proofs for 'The Man Who Died'

1st state

2nd state

3rd state

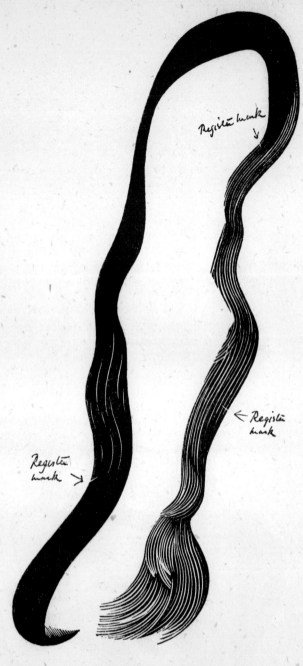

Complete red block for engraving on previous page

Progressive proofs for ' The Man Who Died'

3rd state   *Progressive proofs for 'The Man Who Died'*   1st state

2nd state

Progressive proof and red block for ' The Man Who Died'

Red block

During the summer I made a two-colour lino-cut poster for the G.P.O. After some discussion with the G.P.O. as to a suitable subject, it was decided that I should base my design on a film of Grierson's, showing cables being laid under the City. I went to the small theatre off Tottenham Court Road, where the G.P.O. showed their films, and Grierson ran through some films while I made notes of parts of the film I wanted to see again.

Grierson struck me as being a real artist—he was criticizing his films all the time they were running; more to himself than to me. So often one has looked at pictures while the artist himself is looking at them for faults and learning something from his earlier efforts. I went back into the cutting room and studied the rolls of films, making sketches as I went.

My ultimate design was based on my impression of the whole film. Not one of the stills was a good design; but when the film was running the design of movement was perfect. It was then I discovered the difference in designing for the flat surface of a poster and designing for the movement of a running film. I mounted the lino type high and persuaded the printers to work direct from the lino.

In the September of this year I made a line-drawing that was cut in stone to form a decoration over the mantelpiece of a private house in Beaconsfield. I could not cut the stone myself—which I regretted—and so employed a young sculptor to work under my directions. The design was carried out with a V-cut; a suggestion of modelling was given by rounding off the edges of the line where such roundness was necessary. Some interesting problems arose, such as the effect of light on a cut line, the carrying power of a simple linear design on a plain wall surface, and the marrying of a modern design with period furniture, that gave me plenty to think about.

I intended to learn stone carving at once, so that I could carry out my own designs, but I have never found time to do this. I think every engraver should have the ability to cut or engrave various materials, but I have not yet found the day long enough to do the things that I think should be done.

BOOK-JACKET FOR 'PENNY FOOLISH', BY OSBERT SITWELL (1936)

This wrapper is mentioned because it is a combination of wood-engraving, halftone and photo-lithography. My comments on the possibilities in the mixing of reproductive methods occur elsewhere in this book. I do not often get the chance to experiment with processes owing to the shyness of the publishers (perhaps the expense), but I am sure a whole book could be written on the possibilities, not only of the processes themselves, but the mixing of them. The different processes, like the different colours on an artist's palette, should be looked upon as a means of getting certain effects; if they must be mixed, then mix them; if a new way of using one of the colours is necessary, then use it. Otherwise reproduction becomes a habit, and a dull habit at that.

In the autumn of 1936 I was asked to decorate the wall space of one of the rooms of the Sunday Times Exhibition. With only three weeks to finish the job, I had to think and work fast. It seemed a good reason for using photographic enlargements of small scale designs. These designs were made pell-mell from a huge collection of

2 B

photographs, book-jackets, and odd specimens of objects connected with the book trade. The enlargements were made and pasted up like wallpaper and colour added at the last moment. Adjustment of design was necessary here and there, but on the whole the enlarging idea worked fairly well.

I should not have got this job done without the help of Norman Weaver (who has, incidentally, made the photographs for this book). We worked together, and I believe it was this job that started him off on photo-montage decorations. He has produced some since that are quite masterly in handling, and show what can be done in the way of *décor* for exhibition. I hesitate to talk of such methods of decorations, having so little experience, but if anyone cares to enlarge up a small print or a scale design to the size of a wall, he will discover what I discovered when I enlarged up a Doré, a Bewick, and the designs for the Sunday Times Exhibition. A good design, however small, will enlarge up indefinitely and, incidentally, make good decoration.

'THE GODS HAD WINGS', T. H. BROWN
(1936)

I read this MS. with great pleasure. It combined symbolism, wit, scholarship and a sincere feeling for animal life: what more could an illustrator ask for? I had the forms of the birds with their textures and patterns on which to base my designs; while the symbolism that formed the basis of the book gave my abstractions their direction. The book is a neat example of how an abstract design grows out of a natural form, and my illustrations followed the motive of the book in this respect. The titles were designed to work into the engravings—in some cases the type had to be let into the block. I discovered, too, how important a part texture will play in the significance of motive. A vulture is a loathsome animal and I had to find a loathsome texture.

Early proof for ' The Gods had Wings'

2 B 2

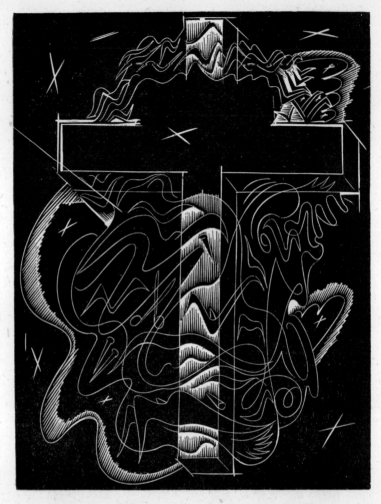

'The Gospel according to the Birds.' Title designed to be set in type and dropped in space on cross.

Early proof for ' The Gods had Wings '

*The Dove is shown in the text as an emblem of spring—it is
shown above in embryo in the bark of a hollow tree.*

Early proof for 'The Gods had Wings'

'A COUNTRY GARDEN', BY ETHEL ARMITAGE
(1936)

One day Carrington asked me if I had engraved flowers.
I told him I had produced one print—'Hemlock'. He
saw it and asked me to do a book of flowers and trees,
and so, after eight years, the 'Hemlock' was to bear
fruit. I was, by now, so interested in the blocks of the
nineteenth century that I was filled with the desire to
engrave my flowers as simply as the garden magazines
of 1860 to 1870. I searched the junk heaps of London and
found a number of these delightful journals that are so
full of serene labour.

In March I paid my first visit to the author in Kent
and drew an oak tree in a biting east wind. During the
year I spent many delightful week-ends in that house in
Kent, with two of the most charming hosts that one can
hope to meet: the charm of the author is in her book; it
tells more of her personality than any words of mine
can, and I followed the seasons as her book follows
them. The engravings show little concern for textures,
except where textures became an essential part of
botanical accuracy. I learned economy of statement by
studying the flowers closely; and simplicity of outlook
from the garden magazines of the past. Some of the
drawings were made in Suffolk while I was on holiday.
I could not travel easily as I was recovering from an
operation, and Carrington's father-in-law—P. F. Alex-
ander—who lived in the neighbourhood, scoured the
countryside and brought in, on one occasion, the very
last Magnolia left in Suffolk, and, on another, a hazel
nut at the great risk of breaking his neck. He was very

triumphant on these occasions and more than helpful. I spent some delightful hours looking at his books, some of which are now in my collection, and talking for hours when we both should have been working.

1st state

2nd state

Progressive proofs for 'A Country Garden'

1st state

Progressive proofs for 'A Country Garden'

2nd state

3rd state

Progressive proof for 'A Country Garden'

I brought back from Suffolk a memory of a man and his wife who have found a good way to live.

In the June of this year, 1936, I lunched with Sacheverell Sitwell, to discuss the making of a book on Old-fashioned Flowers. I was to make some coloured plates in lithography, an experiment fostered by Carrington and Sitwell and one that I looked forward to.

And in the autumn of this year I heard from Macy, of The Limited Editions Club in America:

2nd October 1936

Dear Mr. Farleigh,

I don't know whether you have seen Mr. Bernard Shaw recently, so I am writing to tell you that I saw him at Malvern

*last month, and discussed with him a project for making an
edition of one of his plays to be published through The
Limited Editions Club. We had had a previous correspondence about this project, and he had suggested a new edition of*
Back to Methuselah. *Now he suggests that you might make
the pictures.*

*So I write you this note to learn if you are interested in
making a series of pictures to illustrate a new edition of* Back
to Methuselah. *If you are, I would be grateful if you could
arrange to see Mr. Shaw and to learn for yourself what ideas
he may have about the making of such a book. From his ideas,
you might then be able to prepare a physical plan for the book
and your illustrations.*

*I expect to be at the office of The Nonesuch Press during the
month of November, and would be interested indeed to hear
from you about all this.*

Cordially yours

(Sgd.) GEORGE MACY

Director

It will give an idea as to how long a book will take to
make when I record that the Sitwell plates are just
finished as I write (end of June 1939), and, though I
finished the *Methuselah* engravings last August, I have
signed the colophon sheets this week. I presume both
books will be out this autumn, when this book also is due
to appear—another job that was started two years ago.

TWO POSTERS FOR THE UNDERGROUND
(1937)

My mind was full of flowers, drawn or engraved in
colour, so that when I was asked to make some posters

for the Underground, I suggested the designs should be based on wild flowers and grasses. It seemed to me that a mixture of wood and lithography would give the contrasting qualities of softness and hardness that are so peculiar to plant form. The roughs were passed and I ordered two full-size wood blocks, side grain, and a batch of very attractive cutting tools. The key-drawing was made direct on to the wood. Before I cut I drew the other four colour printings on top of this key and made a tracing of them. The block was placed on an easel and I stood up to what was virtually a piece of wood-carving. I used a knife, V and U-shaped gouges, and hit away happily with a mallet, enjoying to the full the mixture of physical and mental exertion. It is not often one combines these two pleasures—I suppose sculptors do so always. When the key-blocks were cut I offset them on to lino mounted on wood to type height; the second colour, being a fairly simple block, I decided to cut on lino.

The first block was on wood and contained the fine solid lines on a white ground. The second block was on lino and contained all the fine white lines on a solid ground. That is the brief explanation of the selection of the different material. What I could do in wood was not advisable in the softer medium. Thus one's design is partly controlled by the medium, just as the choice of medium is partly controlled by the desired effect.

When the lino and wood was cut for both posters a double offset of the two colours was laid on to zinc, as the three remaining colours were to be in litho. I worked at the Curwen Press with, I fear, only the vaguest knowledge of what I was doing, but full of hope. There

is no doubt that a poster for the Underground is a plum
in the commercial world. It is the nearest thing the
modern artist can get to the decoration of public
buildings that was such common practice at one
time.

I had no final colour sketch to proof by: when it came
to proofing on the machine I had to visualize the effect
I wanted and work blind. This is a mistake on the whole,
but I had worked without a drawing from the very
beginning, and it seemed best to find my way to the
very end and discover what I could from the method as
it progressed. Discoveries are made so much more
readily when the limitations are not set beforehand. I
found myself being influenced by chance effects that I
should have missed had I known exactly what I wanted
beforehand. I repeat that it is not wise to work this way
always, for it is far from economic when proofing and
it is also nerve-racking. When it takes so long to clean
up the machine one needs to make few mistakes in
colour. The first two colours are fairly simple, but it
becomes increasingly difficult to build up to the final
printing. The last colour of all may lead to the discovery
that the first colour is wrong, and that means a whole
day's work wasted; and a day's work on the machine is
an expensive item for the client to face.

However, if one has the nerve, it is worth doing at
least one job in this way: far more is learned by taking a
few risks than by being eternally careful; and if it is
nerve-racking, at least one is alive.

I look back at the posters now and wish I had been
more experimental than I was, for I realize that my
designs were an experiment in reproduction more than

design. The final achievement of all is really a combination of experimental drawing with experiment in reproduction. It is true that the method was suggested by the quality I was after, but I had so much to learn by the way that the design suffered to a certain extent and became less exciting than the method. However, it was worth it: I enjoyed myself, and the posters were not too bad. Perhaps it is expecting too much to think one should be able to like one's past work.

LILITH (1937)

This block is the last large engraving I have made, and after two years I am beginning to want to make another. They are no longer, as they once were, a form of exercise: I must now have something to say before I want to engrave a print on so large a scale. When I look at the prints of the great masters I realize that few of them are really important. They may be lovely things in themselves, but how many of them are as moving as Dürer's 'Melancholia' or his 'Four Horsemen'? So many prints were made because engraving was the only means of duplication; such a reason does not necessarily produce great prints. I am moved even now by the quality of wood or metal, but I do not wish to make prints any longer merely for the sake of indulging this pleasure: I must wait until I feel I have something to say that can only be said in wood before I make a print that has an existence independent of books.

While I was reading the *Methuselah* play and making notes for illustrations, I was concerning myself with the very serious problem of illustrating a play, and this play in particular. There was a deep underlying motive that

I knew could not be represented on the stage, and on that I pinned my hope for illustrations. Words, acting, and *décor,* not even Preface, could fully complete this statement: neither could my illustrations if it comes to that, but at least they could be as much a part of it as the other aspects. I could have kept my designs theatrical, as Gordon Craig did in his *Hamlet* of the Cranach Press, but I felt the play was too full of variety. Realism, allegory and abstraction combine to give an acute sense of birth, life and death, and the struggle of the creative spirit with its puny effort and tremendous achievement.

I saw Lilith as the beginning and the end, and there emerged in my mind a vague image of this effort to live. I felt if I could evolve this motive before I started the book I should be able to grasp the further substance of the plays. And so I started drawing Lilith as a large engraving. It grew day by day from a vague scribble into a curiously complex design, and it was some months before I felt I could engrave it. I do not think I was at any time fully conscious of the motive—it was too elusive. Evolution has no beginning and no end— whether my design is a finished statement I do not know; neither do I see how I can complete a statement of such a motive. Perhaps it is beyond the powers of an artist to define such things, and yet he is for ever trying to do so. Perhaps it is the perpetual struggle of the artist: by the very force that cannot be explained he is moved to attempt an explanation. This is eternity in itself, and so will remain eternity.

CONCLUSION

AND so this book is finished!

It was to have ended differently, but a job will finish itself, just as a picture will discard the artist when it has done with him, or a child its parent. Apart from the need of my nursing through the last stages of production this book has discarded me, in spite of my intention to bring it up to date. I intended to finish with a day-by-day working diary of the *Methuselah* book. It was kept going for the first year and then suddenly torn up. I could not lay myself so bare. There is something of ourselves that must be kept secret: something that cannot be spoken of without we violate ourselves.

I have given what I can: it is not much, but it may be useful to a few, and those few will forgive me for not giving more. Perhaps in twenty years' time I will write the sequel. I may then be wise enough to be able to do what I have failed to do now.

I should like to thank those whose names appear in these pages as having helped me so much. It is they who have made this book. And to thank those whose names do not appear, for they are many, and their influence and help have also made this book. And to thank those who have had the patience to read it to the end, for they also, I hope, will be my friends.

INDEX

INDEX